A Theological Response to Special Economic Zones and Livelihood in India

Christian Heritage Rediscovered

The Series, as the name suggests, is meant to focus on Christian Faith & Living vis-à-vis topics like Literature & Poetry, Indigenous Philosophizing, Ethical response towards Agriculture, Health & Healing, Science & Technology, Ecofeminist Theology, Sociological approach towards Human Rights, Law & Politics, Arts, History of Ideas, Ancient Civilizations, Cultural Contiguity, Religious Cosmologies & Mysticism, Footsteps of famous Theologians, World Peace & Harmony, Global Capitalism, Network Marketing, Cybertheology, Population & Demographics, Epigraphic Studies, Contextualized Education, and many others. We welcome a Mss. on any topic/s mentioned, whether they are original works, scholarly monographs, collections of conference papers, revised dissertations, or translations of historical documents. Through the Series we, the Publishers, are striving to put forward published works that may help Institutions, Academic Bodies, Researchers, Scholars and the World at large in furthering their respective knowledge and understanding on the concerned subject. We welcome your comments on our efforts and further suggestions on how we can foster the upcoming thoughtful theologically grounded books.

Christian Heritage Rediscovered - 13

A Theological Response to Special Economic Zones and Livelihood in India

Thomas M J

CWI

Christian World Imprints(TM)

First Published in 2015 by

Christian World Imprints(TM)
Christian Publishing & Books from India
H-12 Bali Nagar, **New Delhi-110015**
info@christianworldimprints.com
www.ChristianWorldImprints.com
Phone: +91 11 25465925

ISBN-13: 978-93-5148-052-5 ISBN-10: 93-5148-052-6

Cataloging in Publication Data--DK

Courtesy: D.K. Agencies (P) Ltd. <docinfo@dkagencies.com>

Thomas, M. J., 1977- **author**.
A theological response to special economic zones and livelihood in India / Thomas M J
pages cm. -- (Christian heritage rediscovered ; 13)
Includes bibliographical references (pages) and index.
ISBN 9789351480525
ISBN 9351480526

1. Economic zoning--India--Uttar Pradesh. 2. Economic zoning--India--Tamil Nadu. 3. Agricultural laborers--India--Uttar Pradesh--Economic conditions. 4. Agricultural laborers--India--Tamil Nadu--Economic conditions. 5. Economics--Religious aspects--Christianity. I. Title. II. Series: Christian heritage rediscovered ; 13.

DDC 330.9542 23

The maps used in this book are not to scale.

Printed at Chawla Offset Printers

Dedicated to my
Dear Parents (Late) Mrs. Sara John
&
Pr. M. K. John

The Book

The book mainly discusses the pitfalls of dominant economic paradigm, in which one of the major policies that has accelerated neo-liberal economic agenda is Special Economic Zone (SEZ). It brings into limelight the adverse influence of SEZ especially on the livelihood of Small Farmers and Agricultural Labourers. Because of SEZ they can no more have access to land, water & forests which provides them life sustaining products. Based on facts and figures, the author asserts that creation of SEZ in India is mainly at the cost of farming land and livelihood of farming communities.

This book brings out the intensity of the destruction caused through empirical evidences based on the field studies done by the author in two States, Uttar Pradesh and Tamil Nadu. This eye opener research work is meant not only for policy makers but also for lay people to make them understand the negative side of SEZ, though they were introduced for economic growth.

The main agenda of biblical theological understanding of the economy is to ensure livelihood to each and every person. So, the author aims to study the impact of SEZ vis-à-vis biblical theological understanding by supplementing Appendices and providing a detailed Bibliography at the end to amplify the radius of readers' understanding.

The Author

Mr. Thomas M J has completed his Masters (M.Th) in Social Analysis from the Senate of Serampore and another in Social Work (MSW) from SHIATS. He further pursues for his PhD in Social Anthropology from SHIATS.

At present, he is a senior Lecturer in Allahabad Bible Seminary. He is also an Associated Resources Person of the Centre for Dalit and Minority Studies, New Delhi. He has authored a book, *Understanding Social Analysis* (SCEPTRE, Kolkata, 2013). He has also contributed several articles in National and International Journals, and English Regional Newspapers on various theological and social issues.

Foreword

Capitalism repeatedly have met with many death blows in recent past yet with the help of neo-liberal economic policies it is resilient and challenging the ordinary people saying 'who can fight against me?' (Rev.13:1-4). The American Empire and its old and new allies are trying to save the spread of crony capitalism with allits mighty power by sacrificing world resources and people. Former Socialist countries are also equally competing with the market economy believing in the unbridled growth model.The world has proved that the growth model or consumption based economic model investing its belief on GNP and GDP calculation cannot last forever because every growth leaves behind unimaginable amount of waste and irreversible consequences. Therefore, pursuit of degrowth becomes inevitable in our context. The emerging Economy of Degrowth not only questions the development model but also it critiques the entire life style of the present generation.

Mr. Thomas M J search for an alternative over against the dominant neo-liberal economy of our state gains meaning in our context. He extensively analyses the early experiences of Free Trade Zones (FTZ) in India and its feasibility in a larger context. Except the lower class and immediate victims who lost their land, others support FTZ hoping that it will increase economic activity around them. Unless and until people experience the ugly face of the neo-liberal policies they are not able to understand its crudeness. In similar way when some neo-liberal economic models are introduced Indian middle class people are fascinated about it and later they cry over the split milk. The trading community in Tamil Nadu once very happy with online shopping but when they faced direct impact of it the story was different, for instance even crackers are purchased at mass level from the Chinese market. The local production units of crackers face stiff competition with the cheap foreign imports. This has given heavy blow to the small scale cracker and match industries in India. All public sectors including service sectors like banking are reeling under trouble in competing with new foreign banks. We all have to realise that globalisation of market economy will bring happiness to only few industrialists and elites but not all Indians.

We need to be skeptical about the idea of steady or stable state which means the state is under the system of liberal economic policies dancing to the tunes of world economic power structures. In the name of stability, the people are blind to elect Right Wing Governments using democracy as a tool and fall in the trap of vicious circle of modern slavery. Appointment of Ex- IMF economists as advisers to the Indian economic policies in the name of stabilizing the economy is adding fuel to the fire. Such neo-liberal economic fever is inflicting innocent citizens by involving themselves in conspicuous consumerism than opportunity to work and survive. Prime Minister, Narendra Modi's ambition to go for hundred mega cities in India as well as vigorous urbanisation as an opportunity for faster development may increase the growth further adding more to GDP and GNP index but such move will end up in ecologically unsustainable and disastrous situation. We must all realise that the so called growth is encouraged not for the sake of removing poverty or unemployment but for the sake of pride among the nations that we have increased our annual production rate.

While searching alternatives we need to find new meaning in certain areas of our daily activities, such as simplicity, frugality, saving, self-help, cooperatives, adding value to the local quality products etc. Such aspects are helpful in reimagining our vision production for life. So, also we need different working relation and ethics in our own life style. As long as we endorse easy-going life and master-servant relationship, we may not able to come out of the capitalist mind cycle. It is not enough to find alternatives with the present capitalist infrastructures and values and it may not able to find right path for the alternatives. We are searching something beyond growth and development but with determination, life affirmation, sustainability and well being of future posterity. In this journey, I believe the book of Mr. Thomas M J may find rightful place in convincing people who try for an alternative to the dominant economic system.

Rev. Dr. Solomon Victus
Tamil Nadu Theological Seminary
28th October2014

Acknowledgment and Thanks

This book is the result of the encouragement and help from many individuals and organizations to whom I would like to express my gratitude. I am specially thankful to Revd. Dr. Ravi Tiwari, who was then the Registrar of the Senate Serampore for giving me permission to publish my M.Th thesis for the benefit of more readers. Also, I am responsible for the changes title, contents and the opinions expressed in it with all the due permissions required.

I extend my sincere and profound gratitude to Revd. Dr. David Rajendran, my guide and supervisor, for his sincere help, generous support, personal interest, creative insights and timely correction of my papers at every stage of my work. I express my thanks to Revd. Dr. Solomon Victus, Dr. Gabriele Dietrich, Revd. Dr. Bastian Wielenga, Dr. John Jayaharan, and Revd. H. Adlin Regina Bai for their timely advice and guidance. I remain grateful to Revd. John Varghese, Dr. P. B Thomas, Dr. M. T. Cheriyan, Mr. Gopakumar Govinden Nair, Mr. Johnson V. Abraham, Gigi and family, Mathew Thomas, Abraham Kurian and Peter Joy, who extended all help for my studies. I express my thanks to the library staff of TTS, especially DSA. I am very grateful to Aunty Leslene Woodward, who carefully read and corrected my script. I express my thanks to (Late) Dr. Christawati Singh, and my friends Biju K. P, Shahid, Monu, Kamal, Susheel, Mani, and Shanti who provided me all help for my field studies in Moradabad and Madurai.

I express affection and thanks to my father M.K. John, his life and affection is the motivating factor in my life, and sisters Susmitha and Suni, my Brother-in-laws Benny Thomas and Benny Jacob for their love, encouragement, prayer, concern and financial support throughout my studies. I am sincerely grateful to my friends Sam Varghese, Laji Chacko, T. P. Salim Thanka Kumar, Arul Jaba Singh, Sharma Nityanatham, Jayaprakash, Sharad and all DSA friends for their consistent support.

Very special thanks to my good friend Mr. Sudhanshu Kanda and Christian World Imprints for taking all the effort to publish this work.

Above all, I am thankful to God Almighty for giving me all the opportunities thus far to complete this work and I believe God will extend special strength to everyone who suffers for their daily needs.

Preface

"Religion is so often understood as a realm far removed from the concerns of "this world" that it is assumed to have little of practical value to offer on trade and commerce, wages and dividends, investments and rewards. We expect churches, synagogues, (temples) and mosques to have much to say about personal behavior, about matters related to the family and sexuality, about interpersonal dealings and individual spiritual yearnings. But if the discussion is about profits and losses, religious voices are supposed to fall silent. This view is, of course, absurd. It is untrue to history—religious traditions have always had much to teach us about the moral underpinnings of economic systems and the practical rules for making an economy good and just. It also is untrue to human nature—if religions teach us that we are supposed to be moral in all our actions, there is no special exemption for activities in the economic sphere."[1]

The essential nature of human beings is his/her ability to interact with nature and fellow human beings. Our fellow creatures interact in a limited way, but we have special ability to interact and coordinate the natural materials for our purposes. The very purpose of interaction and coordination of our fellow creatures is to fulfill the needs of human beings. The interaction between nature and human

---

1 Rebecca M. Blank and William McGurn, *Is The Market Moral? A Dialogue On Religion, Economics, And Justice* (*Washington, D.C;* Brookings Institution Press, 2004), 1.

beings was limited to within the boundary that is set up as natural law. However, when humanity needs also increased and their interaction shifted to mechanical, then need-driven interaction transformed into want-driven interaction. This shift is the result of the change of humanity's world view. People started to question natural laws and even nature. The very purpose of interaction shifted towards taking advantage of fellow beings and nature. This shift influenced all dimension of human life and one of the most influential dimension of human life is economic life.

Almost all the theological documents in the world carry a message for human interaction. How that interaction should take place not only with one another but also with entire ecological system. However, the greed and self-love destroyed the very ethical principle of interaction. Consequently, one takes advantage against another. The most so called efficient person in the world is a person who takes more advantage against other. We call it as 'development', 'success', iconic figures, etc., however the very principle of Biblical Theology negate this evil structure, which takes advantage against our brothers and sisters. Following pages unravel through empirical research how dominant economy promotes the rich to take advantage against the poor.

"...you shall not oppress one another...(because) I am the Lord your God" (Lev.25:17) - The Bible

Thomas M J
Allahabad

General Introduction

India, after her independence, followed different economic paradigms. The present government follows Neo-liberal economic paradigm for development. Thereby, the government of India promotes export-oriented policies. As part of this initiative, the government introduced Special Economic Zone Act in 2005. Special Economic Zone[1] is a special demarcated area of land, which is owned and operated by corporate houses and private companies. Here, Developers and Manufacturers enjoy innumerable long term benefits from the government in the pretext of attracting foreign capital and modern technology.

On the one side, it was introduced with certain claims. It would boost our economy, it would create lot of employment, and India's Gross Domestic Production would increase through Foreign Direct Investment, etc., and on the other side, there are certain challenges: public revenue losses due to tax exemptions, it would destroy employment in the rural areas, the absence of environmental law causes environmental degradation, and for setting up Special Economic Zone huge amount of land, which is primarily cultivable, is being taken from the farmers with the help of Land Acquisition Act, 1894[2]. Consequently, it displaces many, causes cultural degradation,

1 Hereafter it refers as SEZ

2 In 2013, UPA government is replaced this Act with a new Act, at present BJP government going to replace with certain changes, which undermines social impacts.

and threatens the food security and livelihood base of agricultural communities and tribals. The people who depend primarily on land for their survival protested and opposed the move of government to set up SEZ. Irrespective of the oppositions from the common people, some group of intellectuals, ethicists and social workers, the government of India moves ahead with argument that it is the model for India's development.

As the claims go back and forth between the challenges and increasing the number of SEZs, this research work done in the book has studied the adverse influence of SEZ on the livelihood of Small Farmers and Agriculture Labourers, who are the most affected sections. The livelihood of these communities is constituted by access to resources either as owner, worker, or tenant. Access to resources such as land, water and forest provide them life sustaining products. But, SEZ has denied their access to resources and thus denied access to livelihood means.

As the dominant development paradigm challenges the livelihood of certain sections in the society, it also challenges the biblical theological understanding of economy, which knits together all the sections in the society order the concept of 'household of God,' 'it is the site of livelihood'. In this site no one is expected to be deprived due to lack of livelihood. But ensuring the livelihood is the prime agenda of biblical-theological understanding of economy. Hence, the author addresses this issue from a biblical theological understanding.

To find out the livelihood condition of Small Farmers and Agriculture Labourers before and after setting up the SEZ, and also the possible threat of livelihood if land is taken for SEZ, the author has done field study in two places;[3] Moradabad in Uttar Pradesh, and Madurai in Tamil Nadu. For the data collection the author has used structured questionnaire and non-structured interviews.

Sample survey helped in knowing the differential impact on various groups such as household units, gender, and caste. And also interviews were held with officials in order to know the details of the implementation in the sample area. Besides the empirical studies, library research has been done for knowing government

3 The field study procedure is explained in detail in chapter three.

policies and to find out what happened in other SEZ areas. This includes Literatures (books), Seminar papers, Journals, Periodicals, Government documents etc.

Structure of the book:

The First chapter explains the major economic paradigms after independence in India. Mainly brought under three phases of development and are briefly discussed. It began with an aim of developing 'socialist pattern of society' for that cause the institutional reforms emphasized, and introduced development paradigm 'Import Substitution Industry' followed. Then it shifted towards 'growth plus strategy', in which growth with efficiency in production was emphasized. It further moved towards Liberalization,' where export and import was emphasized. In this phase, for the export promotion, SEZ was introduced. It has certain claims as well as challenges. One of the major challenges is threat to livelihood of Agriculture Labourers and Small Farmers.

The Second chapter mainly deals with the framework of the question of livelihood and framework for analyzing the livelihood question. It mainly looked how some major policies influenced the livelihood of these communities.

The Third chapter the same variable, i.e., livelihood question has been discussed in relation to the policy of SEZ. It is based on the field study of the author.

The Fourth chapter explains how Political Parties, Trade Unions, Indian Chamber of Commerce and People's Movement has responded to the SEZ. It brings the contradicting facts that, all the political parties raise voice for the affected farmer's livelihood but at the same time support neo-liberal economic paradigm, which is the main cause of destroying farmer's livelihood base. But the People's Movement seeks for an alternative paradigm, which upholds the livelihood of farmers.

The Fifth chapter, the livelihood negating policy has been evaluated on the basis of people's economy which is based on biblical theology.

Contents

Chapter I

Origin of Special Economic Zone

Introduction

The Leaders, who fought for the freedom of our country, protested against the forced cultivation of Indigo plants by the colonial rulers. Large chunks of land had to be converted for Indigo plants. After around sixty years, the new generation of leaders introduced a new policy called Special Economic Zone; it acquires the farmer's land for the use of export promoting industrial activities.

This chapter mainly deals with the question-- How did SEZ originate? In order to answer this question, this chapter examines following issues--What are the major phases of development?, How does State exercise their role to make new policies with regard to the phases of development?, As part of the new policy how has the SEZ emerged?, What are the major provisions of SEZ?, How it has been implemented?, and finally, What are the major claims and challenges of this policy?

1.1. The Concept 'Development' and Independent India

On the eve of independence, as a nation our leaders started to face different struggles,[4] which were much longer and harder than acquiring independence. The maintenance of freedom required economic strength. For that they introduced many development policies.

The origin of SEZ is part of current economic paradigm of development. The government has been implementing different developmental paradigms since the independence,[5] which have been influenced by ideological, political and international factors. The important economic developmental phases and its shifts- it does

---

4 The new state India was overwhelmed with large-scale communal warfare and carnage, resulting in some quarter million deaths, vast destruction and loss of property, administration breakdown and chaos and the massive influx of six million refugees. Besides that Million of her rural people suffered under the weight of colonial agrarian structure. VKRV Rao, *Values and Economic Development* (Delhi: Vikas Publications, 1971), 87-89.

5 According to Amiya Kumar Bagchi, there were three streams of thoughts fed the movement of economic development; one was conservative nationalist trend, which looked upon private enterprise as the major instrument of development but which wanted the state to step in wherever private enterprise was inadequate. The second group was an official or technocrat stream which regarded economic planning as an essential adjunct to the effort of administrating and improving the poverty-stricken land. Third group was the leaders who thought economic planning were an essential part of a strategy to construct a socialist society in India. Amiya Kumar Bagchi, "Dialectics of Indian planning From Compromise to Democratic Decentralization and threat of Disarray," in *Industry and Agriculture in India Since independence,* ed. by. T. V. Sathyamurthy (Delhi: Oxford University Press, 1998), 47.

In addition to these, a few group had regard for Gandhian concept of development model, which revolved around humans, their society and nature and their respective and simultaneous development. He emphasized village economy and stressed self-reliance, *swadeshi* and decentralization for building Indian economy; Harijan, The collected Work of Mahatma Gandhi 27th Jan., 1940, New Delhi: Govt. of India1958-1984, pp. 71-130. It doesn't mean that he completely opposed to all kind of mechanization and large scale industry. He was realistic enough to see that some modern development did have a limited role in India's future and this was not to enrich a few or displace labor or produce things villagers could easily produce on a small scale; B. N. Ganguli, *Indian Economic Thought* (New Delhi: Tata-McCraw Hill Pub., 1977), 247.

not deal the political, ideological, and international factors in detail-follow:

1.1.1. Origin of 'Import Substitution'

Soon after the independence, in Nov. 1947, All India Congress Committee[6] defined independent India's broad political objectives and economic programmes in the following terms:

> "Our aim should be to resolve a political system which will combine efficiency of administration with individual liberty and an economic structure which will yield maximum production without the concentration of private monopolies and the concentration of wealth and which will create the proper balance between urban and rural economies. Such a social structure can provide an alternative to the acquisitive economy of private capitalism and regimentation of totalitarian state."[7]

This was the first official statement by the national leadership of the 'third way' in economic development. For that Jawaharlal Nehru, the first Prime Minister of India, adopted the 'Birla Plan.' This plan emphasized the need to modernize traditional society, by making use of the western science and technology and drawing international experience.[8] At the same time, Nehru stressed the object of this is to establish a 'Just Social Order'- 'growth with redistribution,' thereby preventing the growth of economic disparities with the progress of industrialization.

6 Congress was the main representative body planned the economic policies.

7 Indian National congress, *Resolutions on Economic Policy, Programme and Allied Matters -1924-1969* (New Delhi: All India congress Committee, 1969), 18-32. Quoted in Francine R. Frankel, *India's Political Economy, 1947-2004* (New Delhi: Allied Publishers Ltd., 1978), 20.

8 Erik Komarov, *Nehru's Views on History as Society and Politics, Jawaharlal Nehru and Reminiscences and Studies* (New Delhi: Streting Pub., 1989), 47.

In 1950, the government set up a Planning Commission.[9] The Directive Principles[10] in the Constitution are the guiding principles for the planning. In the plan the government emphasized the redistribution of the ownership of resources, i.e., land. Nehru recommended the removal of intermediaries between the tiller and state, the fixation of land ceiling with the surplus land organized in village co-operatives,[11] and also gave priority to agriculture, rural development, irrigation, and power. Regarding the industrial growth, the government suggested tripartite division[12] and emphasized rapid industrial growth by encouraging foreign capital in the beginning.[13]

---

9 "Planning as the instrument of accelerating economic development is concerned with overall strategy of the process of growth, and one of its initial tasks is to specify the goals of economic development over time". The Planning Commission was an advisory body to cabinet and National Development Council. It is a larger body comprises prime minister, other members of the commission and chief ministers of the states. The government has both long term and short term plans. Generally, planning commission set up five years plan to implement the economic policy of the government. C. T Kurian, *Our Five Year Plans* (Bangalore: CISRS, 1966), 47.

10 The citizens, man and women equally, have the right to an adequate means of livelihood, The ownership and control of the material resources of the country are so distributed as best to subserve the common good, The operation of the economic system does not result in the concentration of wealth and means of production to the common detriment.

11 Indian National congress, *Resolutions on Economic Policy, Programme and Allied Matters 1924-1969* (New Delhi: All India congress Committee, 1969), 18-32. Quoted in Baldev Raj Nayar, *India's Mixed Economy* (Bombay: Popular Prakashan, 1982), 181.

12 First, an exclusive monopoly sector for the state (arms and ammunition, railway transport, and atomic energy). Second, reserved Public sector (coal, iron and steel, aircraft manufacture, shipbuilding, telephone and telegraph manufacture, and mineral oils). Resolution did not check the co-operation of private sector. Third, Barring above two sectors rest of the industrial arena remained with private enterprises, whether individual or co-operatives. At the same time state has the right to progressively participate or intervene if necessary Baldev Raj Nayar, op. cit, 183-184.

13 Industrial development had to look back on a century preceding industrial development. Certain characteristics of that development were: some industries which developed during that century were controlled British capital, and some other was by Indian capital. The industries controlled by the foreign capital, such as, jute, tea etc were mostly dependent on foreign markets. But

In the second five year plan the import substitution was shaped, for that Industrial resolution was amended in 1956. In this new Act, the public sector assumed a leading role in the development, at the same time the private sector was given opportunity to develop and expand through the cooperation with public sector. The policy also emphasized the high importance of the growth of cottage, village and small scale industries. In addition to New Industrial Policy, New Company Act was also brought out with the objective of 'socialist pattern of society,'[14] and also government introduced protective measures for the domestic production.

At a policy level, this attempt was to induce industrialization in the country and to generate a climate where capital goods and consumer goods production could effectively substitute imports.

However, due to food shortage, Nehru tried to introduce 'corporate farming,' but it was strongly opposed by the industrialists and rich landlords. Also external pressure on the internal problem of food shortage mainly emphasized more production than any institutional reforms. As a result, food import started and initiated for economic reforms soon after the third plan. In the beginning, it was aimed to supplement the import substitution with export earnings with external assistance.[15] So, the protection of domestic economy was in the forefront of government policy during this period.

Near the end of Nehru's tenure, India faced a serious economic crises. Nehru successors had to face these crises. The first attempt was to shift away from Nehru's policy. However, after the short term of Lal Bahadur Sastri, Indira Gandhi initially adopted some radical steps as part of her economic policies.[16]

---

the industries controlled by the Indian capital depended on Indian market (domestic), Amlan Datta, *An Introduction to India's Economic Development since Nineteenth Century* (Bombay: Popular Prakashan, 1989), 43.

14 Francine R. Frankel, op. cit., 130; C. T. Kurian, *Poverty Planning and Social Transformation* (Bombay: Allied Pub., 1978), 117.

15 Sunanda Sen, "From Import Substitution to Export Promotion: Policy Planning in India's Foreign Trade Sector," *Economic and Political Weekly* 17/14-16 (November, 1982): 630.

16 Some of the major steps were: Bank nationalization:-fourteen banks were nationalized. It was to obtain control over the commanding heights of the economy. Constraining the corporate private sector: - In order to check

However, by late 1973 and through 1974 India was in throes of a grave economic crises.[17] To face this situation, government introduced growth-oriented strategy in which production was aimed to increase.

Nehru's economic policy has been seen differently by different people. For Sanjay Baru, Nehru adopted the paradigm of modern capitalism and state socialism.[18]For E.M.S Namboodiripad Nehru's policy acted as catalyst and helped the growth of capitalism and consequently used state power for this.[19] But Indian Federation of Chamber of Commerce and Industry criticized and protested the policy of the government.[20] Though there are different opinions regarding the economic paradigm which Nehru adopted, it was clear that it aimed for socialist-pattern of development. This effort was partially achieved.

1.1.2. 'Growth Plus Strategy'

In order to tackle the crisis, the government sought the help of external aids. It was on the basis of long term credits. Eventually, the pressure on the balance of payments intensified. It pressurize Indian economy to move towards devaluing the rupee and emphasize export promotional policies.[21] However, the export mainly aimed to assist the

---

and control the big business group, government had taken two steps: One is Monopolies and Restrictive Act, 1969, and second one is Modification of industrial licensing Policy, 1970, both were aimed to check the emerging monopoly of private sector and place public sector on the commanding heights of the economy. After the 1971 election, she had further accelerated radical steps by nationalizing General insurance and coal industry, Indian Iron and steel company, copper and refineries, cotton textile mills, wholesale wheat trade. Baldev Raj Nayar, op. cit., 274.

17 Crisis in relation with Bangladesh, Suspension of economic aid by US, production crisis, sharp jump in oil prices, state policies and poor performance of public sector, etc., see more Ibid., 329-331.

18 Sanjay Baru, "Development Alternative", *Religion and Society*, 43/1&2 (March & June, 1996): 74.

19 E. M. S. Namboodiripad, *Economic and Politics of Indian Socialist Pattern* (New Delhi: People's Publishing House, 1966), 194.

20 See more Francine R. Frankel, *India's Political Economy, 1947-2004,* 223-235.

21 Francine R. Frankel, op. cit., 294.

import substitution, thereby domestic market was being protected. This move was to achieve 'growth (export) with efficiency'[22] or 'growth plus strategy'. This strategy did not emphasis any change in the distribution of the means of production.[23] The major means of production in the Indian economy is land. So, the government made shift from earlier policies during this period.

Meanwhile, Indira Gandhi faced serious oppositions; consequently she imposed an emergency regime on the country.[24] After the emergency, Janata Party took over power for a short period.[25] In 1980, Indira Gandhi returned to power and carried out the policies that she begun in 1974. Liberalization of economy was seen as the ruling principle.[26]

After the death of Indira Gandhi, her son Rajiv Gandhi succeeded her in 1984; when balance of payments financial shortage showed signs of worsening, external borrowing increased. So, he introduced the new policy in which he rarely talked about socialism and intoduced new principles of competition and greater integration with the global economy, which gave more emphasis to private sector, and export oriented production. The reformed trade and industrial policy eliminated licensing requirements for private domestic and foreign investment in certain industries and relaxed

22 Sunanda Sen, "From Import Substitution to Export Promotion: Policy Planning in India's Foreign Trade Sector" *Economic and Political Weekly*, 630.

23 C. T. Kurian, *Poverty Planning ...*, 16-18.

24 Baldev Raj Nayar, op. cit., 328-335; Francine R. Frankel, op. cit., 521-547.

25 The Janata government consisted different political groups so they struggled to maintain political coherence. It reflected their economic policies. They worked out for an alternative economic model which mainly aimed to reduce the rural-urban disparities and promote an agriculture-led economic growth and an employment oriented work programme; promotion of small scale industries etc.,

26 Though planners established the dominant role of public sector in industrial development, it failed to bring out proper growth in the economy—specially, in compare with the industrial growth in East Asian countries—as a result new emphasis was given to export-oriented production. It was also outcome of the loan agreement, mainly to make balance of payment deficits arises from the 1979/80 oil shock and higher costs for growing imports under various liberalization measures with the International Monetary Fund. See Francine R. Frankel, op. cit., 580-585.

the restrictions under the Monopolies and Restrictive Trade Practices Act. Thus, the new policy started to move away from the concept of 'self-reliance.' But in 1989 election, Congress lost power and two coalition governments came into power for the next two years. After that congress returned to power under P. V. Narasimha Rao.[27]

1.1.3. Liberalization

When the new government came into power in 1991, it was said that a serious economic crisis had developed.[28] Under such crisis, the government sought the help of International Monetary Fund, and IMF required macro-adjustment, Structural Adjustment Programmes (SAP), in the economic policy. Prime Minister Rao was backed by his Finance Minister Manmohan Singh and his team to work out package policies that was in line with the demand of IMF and World Bank. The government followed LPG model; Liberalization, Privatization and Globalization.[29] As a result, the industries reserved for public sector were drastically cut back, rupee was devalued, import restriction was taken away, etc., and the same was further accelerated by the successive governments. They implemented many reforms

---

27 Ibid., 585-588; Bhabatosh Datta, *Indian Planning at the Crossroads* (Delhi: Oxford University Press, 1992), 23ff. Sharad Joshi, *Bharat Speaks Out* (Bombay: Build Documentation Centre, n. d.,), 45-53.

28 The total public debt accumulated to 76 percent of GDP, interest payment reached 4 percent of GDP, and 20 percent of the total expenditure of the central government. See more, Francine R. Frankel, op. cit., 590.

29 The essence of liberalization is that economic management should be left to the market. It follows from this that the state should take a back seat in economic matters.

The privatization meant that all public sector economic activities that are in operation should be closed down, phased out, trimmed or passed on to the private sector. Public ownership should be allowed only in cases of natural monopolies and strategic industries.

The core of ideas of Globalization is that more trade is better for all the parties concerned-some may gain more that, but all would eventually gain. Any action that interferes with the free flow of capital, goods and services, would produce sub-optimal results. So, all the protective measures to protect the inward looking economy are to be removed. See more Biplab Dasgupta, *Globalization Structural Adjustment Experience* (New Delhi: Sage Pub., 2005), 20-22.

in the policies: Economic reforms, Foreign policy reforms, Agrarian reforms, etc.,[30] All the planning which government proposed was in line with the recommendations made by the international monetary agencies. The areas controlled earlier by the public sector started opening for the private sector one after another.[31]

Again this policy moved further in relation to World Trade Organization and its laws: Trade-Related Intellectual Property Rights (TRIPS), and Trade-Related Investment Measures (TRIMs), through which multinationals could invest (Foreign Direct Investment) in member countries. Under TRIMs, WTO member countries cannot impose any of these restrictions on the investors (foreign or domestic). Thus, India's industrial policy got influenced by TRIMs. Another law called Agreement on Agriculture (AoA) took away the barriers so as to allow trade in agriculture products. Non-Agriculture Market Access (NAMA) elimination of Tariff on industrial products helped rich nations to produce goods at the cost of cheap labour in the poor countries.[32] Thus, it reached another extension of liberalization, i.e., Neo-liberalization.

There was technological revolution during this time, with an unprecedented surge in Information Technology sector. The information technology was given higher priority than industrial production. So the main vision was to unleash an information technology surge through Indian technologically educated class.[33] But, there was need of creating world-class infrastructure in order to compete internationally. There were various proposals, such as 'Island of excellence' and Special Economic Zone, that were put forward in order to establish a world class infrastructure.[34]

Thus, the economic development which once started with an aim to create socialist pattern of society and its essence was Import

---

30 See more, Jos Mooij, *The Politics of Economic Reforms in India* (New Delhi: Sage Pub., 2005), 18-25.

31 Francine R. Frankel, op. cit., 590.

32 T. K. Bhaumik, *The WTO: A Discordant Orchestra* (New Delhi: Sage Pub., 2006), 36-40, 100.

33 T. K. Bhaumik, *The WTO: A Discordant Orchestra* (New Delhi: Sage Pub., 2006), 36-40, 610.

34 Ibid., 611-622.

Substitution Industries and institutional changes was later moved to Export-oriented Production without any protective measures to domestic economy. Consequently, to create a feasible atmosphere to work out market principles and export-oriented growth SEZ was introduced.

1.2. Changing Role of the State

A developmental ideology was a constituent part of the self-definition of the post-colonial state. The state was connected to the people-nation not simply through the procedural form of representative government, but also it asserted its representativeness by directing a programme of economic development on behalf of the nation. But the two criteria of representativeness and hence of legitimacy could well produce contradictory implications for state policy.[35]

According to Sukhamoy Chakravarty, in the planning and implementation of policy state fails when: (a) the planning authorities are inefficient in gathering the relevant information, (b) they take so much time to respond that the underlying situation has by then changed, and (c) when the public agencies through which the plans are to be implemented do not have the capacities to carry them out and the private agencies combine in strategic ways to disrupt the expectations about their behavior.[36] By looking at these three factors with regard to above discussed three phases, we can understand the role of the state. The first two factors can be seen in different levels in every phases of Indian economic development. But the third factor mainly defines the role of the state, and reason for changing the role of the state. This third factor influenced the role of the state differently in these three phases of economic development.

In the first phase, i.e., 'Import-Substitution', as per the Industrial policy resolution of 1956, all the key sectors were controlled by the

---

35 Partha chatterjee, "Development Planning and the Indian State", in *State and Politics in India,* ed. by Partha Chatterjee (Delhi: Oxford University Press, 1998), 276.

36 Sukhamoy Chakravarthy, *Development Planning: The Indian experience* (Oxford: N.p, 1987), 40-42, cited by, Partha chatterjee, op. cit., 276.

public sector.[37] During this time there was less private agencies' interference. State was in a position to implement ideologically motivated policies to build 'socialist pattern of society'. It was aimed to protect domestic economy.

In the second phase, i.e., 'Growth-Plus Strategy', the state was welfare state. But, as it received aid from external agencies, state deliberately had to make some policy arrangement so that export would be promoted and foreign exchange earned. That would help state to repay long term credits payments. However, it was mainly to assist the domestic economy.

In the third phase, 'neo-liberalization', onwards a change occurred in the role of the state, mainly due to the policy change. Private sector increased remarkably between 1978 and 1982. There were many joint-sector groups also set up during this time. The apex body of these business groups was the Federation of Indian Chamber of Commerce and Industry, and the Associated Chambers of Commerce and Industry, which gradually obtained the power to bargain and influence the governmental policies. Business interests in India focus their attention on executive agencies rather than Parliament, which plays a limited role in the formulation, choice, and implementation of policy. Their political influence and contributions to the political parties, who form government, was invisible but important channel of influence. But, later it was more visible.[38] Other than this private sector influence, there were international agencies like IMF, WB, and WTO[39] which influenced the functioning of the state when they approach for help during the crisis time. State sought structural adjustment loan first in 1981. After that in 1991, there was full-fledged move for a loan from IMF. Government began fulfilling 'anticipatory conditionalities,' including two successive devaluations

37 C. T. Kurian, *The Economy Interpretative Introduction* (Madras: Sage Pub., 1992), 360; Lloyd I. Rudolph and Susanne Hoeber Rudolph, *In Pursuit of Lakshmi: The Political Economy of The Indian State* (Bombay: Orient Longman Ltd.,1987), 23.

38 Ibid., 30-32.

39 All these organizations are controlled by the rich countries who act in favour of the TNC's and MNC's

and withdrawal of export subsidies. [40] Thus, Indian policy started to be controlled in different ways by these agencies; as a result state became an instrument of these organizations. Eventually, state was forced to move away from the concept of 'welfare state' and social welfare was left to the market. During the neo-liberalization era, state was totally influenced by the business lobbies as well as by the market. So, the main function of the state was only to create a suitable atmosphere for global market, to function consequently they adopted many policies, which promote the interest of the big cooperative houses. Promotion of SEZ is one among them.

1.3. The Emergence of the Concept 'Special Economic Zone'

The forerunner of SEZ is Export Processing Zone (EPZ),[41] the first of which came into being in Shannon, Ireland in1958.[42] The history of SEZs in India suggests that the seeds of the basic concept of SEZ were sown at Kandla in the year 1965. Thereafter, some other EPZ also started in India. EPZ created privileged zone with liberal tax and labour regimes with less social security for workers to attract investors from developed Countries by allowing them to take advantage of cheaper costs and fewer regulations to set up manufacturing units that could import materials for use in manufacturing products for export.[43] Shankar Gopalkrishnan distinguishes three types of Zone policies;[44]

Firstly, 'Zones are part of an export oriented development strategy.' These zones, which were established in 60s and early 70s, instituted as an alternative import substituting industrialization that was the norm of most developing nations. This strategy aimed at industrial development through careful stimulation of certain types

---

40 Wayne Ellwood, *The Non-nonsense Guide to Globalization* (Cornwall: TJ International, 2005), 27-31; Biplab Dasgupta, op. cit., 18, 52.

41 Hereafter it refers as EPZ.

42 Sangita Mulgi, "Special Economic Zone," *Lawyers Collective* (October, 2006): 5.

43 Sangita Mulgi, "Special Economic Zone," *Lawyers Collective* (October, 2006): 5.

44 Shankar Gopalakrishnan, "Signs of an Impending Disaster," *Seminar* 582 (February, 2008): 26-30.

of export. However, repression of labour and consequently low wages was the fearsome factors of these zones. EPZs in India, like some other countries, were introduced for increasing exports and addressing the increasing foreign exchange that would expectantly enrich import substituting industrialization.

Secondly, 'Zones as a crisis response.' Here zones are established as a response to failure of the overall economic strategy. As import-substituting industrialization collapsed before the neo-liberal economies, the need for foreign exchange shifted to generalized requirement to promote exports. First type of export was the means to get foreign exchange. Now export became the end itself. These zone policies essentially revolved around repression of labour, tax concessions, elimination of tariffs and tax regulation. Such zones attracted capital desiring unskilled, cheap labour with high levels of industrial mobility. This type of zones reflected the dominance of international capital over labour.

Thirdly, 'Zones as new arenas for capital'; this type of zone was established firstly in China. These zones allowed for foreign investment, contract labour, more decentralized economic management and other reforms. These changes took place over against the backdrop of socialized command economy without private property, contract labour or market forces.

In China, since the late 1970s, and especially since the 3rd Plenary Session of the 11th CPC Central Committee in 1978, the People's Republic of China (PRC) government decided to reform the national economic situation and open it to the outside world.[45]

As part of economic reform during the 1980s, the People's Republic of China established SEZs and open coastal cities and areas, and designated open inland and coastal economic and technology development zones.[46]

45 Bhaskar Goswami, "Special Economic Zones: Lessons from China" URL: htt p://en. wikipedia.org /wiki/Special_Economic_Zones_ of_the_People's_Republic_of_China as retrieved on 18 Jun 2008 03:18:03 GMT.

46 Ibid.

The main purpose for SEZ is to act as 'windows' in developing foreign oriented economy, thus generating foreign exchange by boosting exports and importing advanced technologies. This helped China to improve the coastal regions and thus accelerate the development of these regions. Since its founding in 1992; the Shanghai Pudong New Zone has made great progress in both absorbing foreign capital and accelerating the economic development of the Yangtze River valley.[47]

However, it gradually ceased to be an exporting center and became the center of capital accumulation. And rapid accumulation becomes the goal of state action. So, they made law for grabbing the land for setting up the Zones. It eventually led to the explosion in real estate speculation.[48] And also, the rapid growth of the coastal regions of China did not get transmitted to the provinces of the hinterland. As consequences a divide has emerged between the rich and affluent coastal regions and the hinterland in China.[49]

According to Shankar Gopalakrishnan, this type of zone "became instruments for reshaping the state machinery itself and generating a new relationship between the state, capital and other sectors of society."[50]

Against this background, it becomes increasingly clear that Indian SEZs belong to the third category. And also the government affirmed that China's SEZ and its influence on economy shows a model. So, a new policy element was introduced in the Exim policy effective from April 2000 for setting up of SEZ. Then after much discussion 'The Special Economic Zone Act, 2005' was passed by the

---

47 Ruddat Datt, "Special Economic Zones,' *Mainstream* 44/47 (Nov., 10-16, 2006): 16.

48 Huang and Yang, "The Political Dynamics of Regulating Change: Speculation and Regulation in the Real Estate Sector," *Journal of Contemporary China* 5 (July, 2006): 12. Cited in Shankar Gopalakrishnan, "Negative Aspects of Special Economic Zones in China," 29.

49 Ibid. see more Shankar Gopalakrishnan, "Negative Aspects of Special Economic Zones in China," *Economic and Political Weekly* 42/17 (April 28, 2007):1492-1494.

50 Shankar Gopalakrishnan, "Signs of an Impending Disaster," 30.

Parliament in May 2005.[51] And SEZ Rules became effective from 10th February 2006. The SEZ Act 2005 defines the key role for the State Governments in Export Promotion and creation of Infrastructural Facilities.

1.4. Special Economic Zone Act, 2005: Overview of the Main Provisions[52]

Any person, a state government or the central government can either jointly or independently set up a SEZ for one of the following purposes:

- For manufacturing of goods
- For rendering prescribed services; or
- As a free trade and warehousing zone.

Any person who intended to set up a SEZ, may, after identifying the area, make a proposal to the state government concerned for the purpose of setting up the SEZ.

SEZ can be of the following types:

1. Multi product SEZ: this is a SEZ where units may be set up for manufacture of goods or rendering services of two or more goods or services in sector, or goods/services falling in two or more sectors.
2. Sector specific SEZ: this is a zone set up exclusively for one or more products or services.
3. Port/Airport based SEZ
4. Free Trade and Warehousing Zone

Each class of SEZ may have different minimum area and terms and conditions set out in the rules (The minimum area for a multi product SEZ is 1000 hectares whereas the minimum area for a free trade and warehousing zone is 40 hectares).

---

51 "Special Economic Zone," *Lawyers Collective* (October, 2006): 5. This was followed after the visit of commerce minister and his team to china in order to learn the development of SEZ there.

52 The Gazette of India (extraordinary Part-II-section I), *Special Economic Zones* (Ministry of Law and Justice), 2005.

Administration and Approvals: Any proposal for setting up of SEZ in the private/ joint/state sector is to be routed through the concerned state government who, in turn, is to send it with its recommendations to the central government–appointed Board of Approval. For each SEZ, the Board of Approval appoints a Development Commissioner who is in overall charge of the Zone and who head an approval committee.

Proposals for setting up SEZs will be judged according to the following criteria:

- Generation of additional economic activity
- Promotion of exports of goods and services
- Promotion of investment
- Creation of employment opportunities
- Development of infrastructure
- Maintenance of sovereignty of India

In order to be located in a SEZ, a unit must be approved by the SEZ Unit Approval committee, which comprises the Development Commissioner, customs authorities and representatives of the state government. The performance of the SEZ units must be monitored annually by the unit Approval Committee and units are liable for penal action under the Foreign Trade (Development and Regulation) Act if the approval conditions are violated.

The Act provides provisions for single window clearance and fast track approval for all future project proposals. These special zones will be treated as they are foreign territories within India.

The SEZ unit and developers will get 100 percent exemption from income tax for 5 years. Further, 50 percent of their ploughed back profits will also be exempted from tax for five years. Foreign direct investment will be permitted automatically and the current regulatory restrictions on townships, housing, built-up infrastructure and construction development do not apply to foreign investment in SEZs.

SEZ units are required to be Net Foreign Exchange (NFE) earners within a period of 5 years from commencement of business.

SEZ units will not have any minimum export obligation.

SEZ units are permitted to provide contract manufacturing services to foreign principals.

Offshore Banking units and international financial services centers may be set up in a SEZ.

SEZs will have their own designated courts and enforcement agency for investigation of civil claims and trial of offences committed in SEZs.

The Act provides for the constitution of an Authority for each SEZ with a view to provide greater administrative, financial and functional autonomy to these zones. The authority will establish fund, which can receive grants and loans from the central government.

Authorized operations which were previously specified in the SEZ rules are made generic and include activities that have been approved either by the central government or by the Development Commissioner of a SEZ.

1.5. Implementation of SEZ: Agitation and Violence

The promotion of SEZs stirred unrest across the country starting from farm lands. Lakhs of people from the far-flung state such as Haryana, Orissa, Uttar Pradesh, Maharashtra, Goa, Tamil Nadu, and West Bengal have been protesting against the SEZ policy.

There are ample evidences which show the violence which occurred in relation to the implementation of SEZ at various places. In Orissa, at Kalinganagar tribal people facing eviction from their home and land, agitated by blocking the road. On Jan 2, 2006, they were fired on by the police eventually 13 tribal people were killed along with two policemen.[53]

In Maharashtra, farmers continually agitated against the unjust acquisition of their land. These agitations focus attention on the potential massive displacement of people from agriculture areas. They have also raised questions about the kind of land being acquired for the SEZs and whether the displaced are getting compensation.[54] The

53 Prafulla Das, "Rural Resistance: Tribal Ire," *Frontline* 23/20 (October 20, 2006): 11-12; Pannala Surana, "Agriculture land Not to Used for N. A Purposes," *Janata* 61/6 (March 19, 2006): 6.

54 Venkitesh Ramakrishnan, "Conflict Zones,' *Frontline* 23/20 (October 20, 2006): 4. In Mumbai reliance Industries Ltd., acquires land just outside

farmers opposed land acquisition and protested against the seizure of their land in Mann (Pune District, in Maharashtra) had to face police bullets on October 6, 2006.[55]

The most striking incident occurred at Nandigram in West Bengal, where a proposal has been made to set up mega-chemical hub and multi-product SEZ. Most of the farmers opposed this move as a result they were threatened by the local leaders of the ruling party in the state. The preliminary report by the All India Independent Fact Finding Team stated that, on 14th March 2007, as the villagers at Sonachura and Gokulnagar[56] were engaged in reading the Quran and performing puja, mostly women and children were in the forefront, believing that they were protected by God, police entered in the village and fired the tear gas and rubber bullets; they continued firing 24 hours. There was large scale looting, burning of the village housing and property and raping reported by the local people. Findings also presented all the evidences which showed that it was a planned attack by the ruling party leaders through the state police.[57] Despite this, West Bengal chief minister in his report to the state assembly noted that the villagers provoked the police and eventually it led to violence.[58]

Acording to P. Rajendran,[59] In Tamil Nadu, caste issue has been stirred-up and used for dividing the people's agitation against SEZ. Eliyampetti and other five villages in Madurai District were marked for SEZ. However, the farmers and agriculture labourers

---

Mumbai. Farmers have been served acquisition notices for the 35,000acres of land. Company claimed it as unproductive land, but people say that we are twice blessed in a year. They have been protesting against this attempt. Dionne Bunsha, "Rural Resistance," *Frontline* 23/20 (October 20, 2006): 9-10.

55 Ibid., 4.

56 Two villages in Nandigram district.

57 All India Independent Fact Finding Team, "Nandigram Violence, preliminary Report," *Janata* 62/9 (March 25, 2007): 8-9.

58 Statement made by West Bengal chief Minister, "Buddhadeb Bhattachajee in the state assembly on March 15, 2007," *Janata* 62/9 (March 25, 2007): 10-11.

59 Interview with P. Rajendran, Organizer of Madurai District Agriculture Workers Union, Madurai, 25 February 2009; Interview with M. Shanti, Pennourmai Iyakkam Member, Madurai, 10 March, 2009.

started to protest against this with the help of political parties and independent unions, mainly AIDMK, and PMK, and *Madurai Mavatta Vyasaya Thozhilali Sangam* (Madurai Agriculture Workers Labour Union). But the local caste problem between *Valayar* or *Muppanar* community and *Parayar* community in the Eliyarpetti village was effectively manipulated by DPI and DMK. The *Valayar* community owned land in the area which was marked for SEZ, and also most of the *Valayars* allied with AIDMK. The *Parayars* are mostly agriculture labourers of this place. They were protesting against SEZ. This issue increased by filing case against *Valayar* who were alleged to be teasing the *Parayar.* So, the police entered this village and attacked the *Valayar* community. The very next day the statue of *Valayar* leader garlanded with sandal. They accused *Parayars,* in reality the police force were covering all area. It further spread out to all other villages and interrupted the struggle against SEZ. Otherwise, the ruling party and other could have effectively use the minor caste problem between these two communities who are either as an owner or worker in the land so as to stop the resistance against SEZ. Generally, by looking at many of these incidents related to the implementation of SEZ, it is clearly evident that implementation of SEZ is accompanied by violence.

1.6. Special Economic Zone: Claims and Challenges

1.6.1. Major Claims

- It generates more production, so SEZ has become a strategy at the centre for ensuring the continuation of a 9% rate of growth of economy.
- SEZs are to be the nucleus of new investment, especially Foreign Direct Investment, jobs and greater exports. Thus, SEZs can be a solution to the country problems.
- SEZs will accelerate development and create a large number of jobs.[60]
- It is suggested that there are backward and forward linkages of industry so it will promote development.

60 The commerce ministry claims that SEZ would generate 44,000 lakhs plus employment over the next ten years.

- Increased production will result enhanced tax collections.
- It is argued that less than 0.1% of the arable land will be involved in the proposed SEZs so this will hardly affect total food production.[61]

1.6.2. Major Challenges

- The union ministries of finance, commerce and industry are in conflict. Finance ministry has been strongly opposing any relaxation in the number of SEZs because it would lead to revenue loss of 100,000 Cores as tax sops.[62] It may eventually lead to cutting down of many programmes for the benefit of common man.
- The bribes that would be earned by the politicians and the profits that would be earned by the developers were source of discontent.[63]
- The transfer of prime agricultural land to non-agricultural activity would affect adversely the socio-economic condition of rural community. There will be a huge demographic shift from village to cities, and rural people become refugees in their own land.[64]
- It is feared that by going in for grabbing unnecessarily large amount of land the developers intend to use the SEZ as a plot for developing real estate business.[65] According to a clause in the SEZ Act (section 5 (2)), as much as 75% of the area under large SEZs (above 1000 hectares) can be used for non-industrial purposes. So, it is most likely the land acquired by private developers will be used for the real estate business.

---

61 Arun Kumar, "SEZ: One more Anti-Bharat Act by India", *The Rally* (May, 2007): 17.

62 See more Kamal Nayan Kabra, "Special Economic Zones," *Mainstream* 44/44 (October 20-26, 2006): 7-8.

63 Ila Patnaik, "Special Zone Called India," *The New Indian Express* (Madurai), January 20, 2007, 8.

64 Kamal Nayan Kabra, "Special Economic Zones," 7-8.

65 Ibid.

- It threatens the food security as the area under cultivation is moved out of agriculture. The report of citizens' research collective shows that the total area under SEZs in 20 states across India is expected to be over 200,000 hectares. This land is capable of producing close to one million tons of food grains.[66]
- The growth of employment since the inception of the reforms in 1991 has been negligible. 60% of the SEZs are in information technology which provides only limited number of jobs. Furthermore the working condition; poor wages, long working hours, and occupation hazards and so on, in existing places like Noida, under which people are employed inevitably, thereby, violating human rights. SEZ would keep the benefits of growth away from the poor.[67] It is reported that around one-third of Chinese zone workers received less than minimum wage.[68] Also in many cases those who get employment end up in menial jobs as contract labourers, and they are governed by "hire and fire policy". In most of the existing zones in India young women between the age of 18-30, constitute the majority of the workforce. Most often they are engaged in the lowest category jobs. They are denied basic rights, such as maternity leave and benefits, crèches, etc., and also unhealthy working environment affect badly the health of these workers.[69]

---

66 Citizens Research Collective, *SEZ and Land Acquisition: Fact Sheet for an Unconstitutional Economic Policy* (New Delhi: Citizens Research Collective, 2008). Cited in "Factfile, SEZs: Frequently Asked Questions," *Seminar* 582 (February, 2008): 15.

67 Ibid., 16.

68 Kankesu, Jayanthakumaran, "Benefit-Cost Appraisal of Export Processing Zones: A Survey of the Literature," *Development Policy Review* 21 (Oxford: Blackwell Publishing, 2003): 1. cited in "Factfile, SEZs: Frequently Asked Questions," *Seminar* 582 (February, 2008): 29.

69 M. Suchitra, "Prospects for Labour," *Seminar* 582 (February, 2008): 36-38.

- SEZs violate the law.[70] It violates the letter and spirit of the India Constitution (see especially Clauses 49 and 51).

It infringes the fundamental rights of the citizen guaranteed in Part III of the Constitution, and either relaxes or makes inapplicable many labour laws.[71]

Environment (Protection) Act is inapplicable to SEZs. No environmental clearance is needed. And also it violates Panchayat Raj Act (1996) for local self government.

It violates laws which grant rights and control to *Adivasi* communities over their land. And it violates many international conventions on human rights.

- Threat to access to water.[72] The Zones will tap ground water in huge quantities it will have disastrous influence on the nearby villages.
- Another major threat is displacement and loss of livelihoods; the findings of Citizens Research Collective's estimate reported that;

> "close to 114,000 farming households (each household on an average comprising five members) and an additional 82,000 farm working families who are dependent upon these farms, which has taken for SEZ, for the livelihood will be displaced...and the total loss of income to the farming and the farm worker families is at least Rs. 212 crore a year. This does not include other income lost (for instance of artisans) due to demise of local rural economies."[73]

---

70 'SEZ and Land Acquisition": Fact Sheet for an Unconstitutional Economic Policy, *Citizens Research Collective*. Cited in "Factfile, SEZs: Frequently Asked Questions," 19.

71 Including labour law under the Industrial Disputes Act, Contract Labour Act, Factories Act Minimum wages Act, and Trade Union Act.

72 See more, "The SEZ Threat to Water and Food Security," *Dams Rivers and People* 5/3 (April, 2007): 2-4.

73 "SEZ and Land Acquisition": Fact Sheet for an Unconstitutional Economic Policy, *Citizens Research Collective,* New Delhi. Cited in "Factfile, SEZs: Frequently Asked Questions," 16.

- The Government of India claims that SEZ will be set up in waste land. But, land classification in India is complex: compartmentalization of land into the categories waste and agricultural is not easy. Both these classification have numerous layers within them. Waste land can be land with scrub, grazing land, pasture, land on which shifting cultivation is carried out of or even agriculture land locked within a notified forest (India has 55.2 million ha of wastelands). There are also issues of people- the poorest, most marginalized in the most backward states- who depend for day-to-day survival on these very waste lands. Most of these lands provide firewood, fodder and other minor forest produce so, most of the land classified by the government as waste is actually common property resources.[74]

The centre government's survey of common property resources speaks of the rural populations depending on them. According to the 54th round of national statistical organization survey,[75] about 15% of India's geographical area is common property resource. And many rural households depend on them. As far as grazing goes the survey added that 56% of rural households reported having livestock, 20% of households depended on common property resource land for grazing and 13% collected fodder from it. The data also showed that the smallest villages were most dependent on common property resources for their livelihood.

Therefore, the land, which is the source of livelihood of the majority of the farming communities, if taken away for SEZ, will adversely affects these communities.

Conclusion

SEZ originated as a result of liberalizing the economy. Eventually, state has become an agent or implementer of the policy in favour of the business class. The main purpose of SEZ is to boost export-

74 "Not Wasted," *Down To Earth* (Nov. 15, 2006): 26.

75 Ibid.

oriented growth. It has been implemented on many occasions forcefully, without having consensus of farmers who are the real owners of agriculture land. However, it has many claims that are to be proved, at the same time many challenges as well, which are already visible. One of the major challenges that already raised by many is its adverse impact on livelihood, specially the livelihood of Agriculture Laboures and Small Farmers. Their livelihood claim has been challenged by the different economic policies of the government. It is discussed in following two chapters.

Chapter II

Significance of Employment and Access to Livelihood in India

Introduction

Majority of Indian population depend on agriculture for their livelihood. The majority among them are Agricultural Labourers and Small Farmers. So, the politico-economic policies which relate to land and agriculture affect them differently. This chapter explains the framework of livelihood question and also the framework for analysis in which this question is discussed, in relation to the major socio-economic policies, such as Land Reform, Green Revolution, and Contract farming.[76]

2.1. Question of People's Access to Employment and Livelihood

Livelihood is the existential dimension of life. It is a means of making a living or means of supporting life. It connects access to resources,

76 Chapter three will be discussing the question of livelihood in relation to the policy of SEZ in particular.

occupation or work and market. It is a multidimensional concept and also not very easy to list out. But for the agriculture sector, land and access to it either as owner, tenant and labour are the basic factors in the formation of a livelihood.

Livelihood of Agriculture Labourers and Small Farmers is constituted by following components; access to resources (land, water forest, and livestock) either as owner or employee, i.e., agriculture labour. The relation of owner to resources, and employee to employer and his/her resources are organized in the society by organizing agency/ies through policies.

Firstly, the access to resources is meant as access to use the resources such as land, water, forest, etc. Livelihood of people change when access to resources change. Land owning farmers have access to land resources. Specially, Small Farmers who hold only small area of a land use it for their needs. Resources include both common land or private land, cultivable land or waste land. Common land or waste land is usually used for grazing domestic animals, which are the sources of livelihood of rural communities. Most of the so-called waste land is the grazing land for these communities.

Secondly, Livelihood consists in access to employment or work. M. Douglas Meeks says that "Work ...is a means of access to (local or global) household and a means of shaping the (local or global) household".[77] And how members of household relate to each other is decided by the organizing agencies in the society; who gets what kind of work? Who owns the tools and product of work? The way a community understands, distributes, and controls work will decide who will have access to livelihood. Therefore, how these organizing agencies view labour or work affects the person who is linked with labour power.

For Agriculture Labourers, employment or work provides access to resources obtaining benefits from it, either as money or objects. It is possible through the relationship between employer and employee. Employee sells his/her labour power to the employer, who combines the resources and labour. The labour power of Agriculture Labourers is an inherited skill. Their work depends on their interest

---

77 M. Douglas Seeks, *God The Economist: The Doctrine of God and Political Economy* (Minneapolis: Fortress Press, 1989), 127.

and attachment to the land. Their employment provides them leisure time. Many depend on family labour. It provides them good number of working days. But, the policy of organizing agency, i.e., the State, decides the nature of this work.

So, the change of ownership of resources and use pattern affect the livelihood of farmers especially Small Farmers. Also the resources use and ownership changes will affect the employment of Agriculture Labourers; their skill, working days, place of work, family labour, time etc.

The policies related to resources (land, water, and forest) and employment have influence on the livelihood of people. The livelihood question--specially in relation to resources (land, water, forest, and livestock) and employment--of Agricultural Labourers and Small Farmers is addressed differently by the organizing agency, State, and other influencing agencies.

2.2. Framework for Analysis

For the analysis of the question of livelihood in relation to these policies, in general, the researcher has used Analytical Descriptive method of C.T. Kurien, which is explained in his book, *The Economy: An Interpretative Introduction.*[78] In this Book, he explains that there are different types of economies that can be seen in the history; rudimentary type, village economy, capitalist economy, and post capitalist (Socialist) economy. He says that the process of evolution and transformation of economy does not imply that later types of economies immediately and totally replace the former. On the contrary, the chances are that there will be considerable overlapping of the different types and for fairly long periods too. So, within this complex framework of an economy he identifies different units. He designates them as 'households' (h); (h-1), self sufficient producer. (h-2), subsistence farmer, household which are not self sufficient having interaction with others. (h-3) market-oriented farmers; household with financial resources and labour, (h-4) household with only labour, (f) firms or enterprises, (m) merchants, (b) financial intermediaries or banks, and (s) state. These units interact with each other. He points out that "a national economy consists of a number

78 C. T. Kurien, *The Economy...*, 225-236.

of heterogeneous units with a variety of links among them" and calls the link between these units as activity chains. The activity chains themselves are overlapping and interacting. These household units are together linked to different circuits; it can be local, national, and global. So, the changes that come out in an economy are the result of changes taking place outside the units (local circuit, national circuit, and global circuit) as well as within the units, and the way in which the two interact.

Here, the researcher's analysis mainly looks at the changes of the interaction of three units (h-2, subsistence farmers, h-3, market oriented farmer, and h-4, Agriculture labour) which is due to the change of (s) state unit's policies, here it is Land Reform, Green Revolution, and Contract Farming.

In his definition of economy C. T Kurien says "economy is a structure of relationship among a group of people"[79] through relationship they enter for the purpose, i.e., Three basic functions of an economy: exercise control over resources, combine resource and labour in production and they decide on the claims of members on the produce.

This analysis makes an attempt to explain the role of these four units (h-1, h-2; self sufficient and subsistence farmers, h-3; market oriented farmers; h-4; Agriculture Labourers) on these three basic functions of economy, and how these functioned in relation to their livelihood.

2.3. Issue of Land: Agricultural Labourers and Small Farmers

During the first three five year plans, India's approach to agriculture development was characterized by two goals: the economic aim of achieving maximum increases in agriculture output to support rapid industrialization; and the social objective of reducing disparities in rural life. In the words of Frankel it is "irreconcilable goals."[80]

79 C. T. Kurian, *The Economy…*, 20.

80 Francine Frankel, *India's Green Revolution: Economic Gains and Political Costs* (New Jersey: Princeton University Press, 1971), 3.

2.3.1. Land Reform and Livelihood

Access to resources can be made possible only by redistributing ownership right of resources to the people. So, the Land Reform was mainly aimed to redistribute the land so that access to land resource is possible to the majority of Indian population.

In the pre-independent India due to political, economic and cultural exploitation the land resources were accumulated and controlled by the upper caste. Mainly, the lower caste people remained landless agricultural wage labourers. In the colonial period, British East India Company, on the one side, recognized exclusive property rights of zamindars and, the *zamindari* system of land tenure extended over forty percentages of British India, and on other side, slightly more than half of the British India a *ryotwari*[81] settlement was introduced. Besides, in some places *mahalwari* system introduced. However, the cultivators depend on money lenders for the credit at the time of crop failures or drought time. Credit was given to them on the security of Land holdings. Eventually, many use to loose their land as they were not able to pay back the debts and money lenders became the landlords.[82] Many of the labourers were exploited and made into forced labour due to debt. Hence, the livelihood concerns of certain sections were stirred up along with independent struggle.

The first peasants' association (later it is called *All India Kisan Sabhas*), which had taken up the livelihood issue of Small Farmers and Agriculture Labourers, was started in Andhra Pradesh by N.G. Rangha. Later in many States peasant association came up and joined together as AIKS. They supported Congress in the political struggle for independence, but always strove to commit the national leadership to an open break with large landholdings and industrialists.[83] They drafted an *All-India Kisan Manifesto* claiming to represent the small land owners, tenants, and landless labourers. "The Minimum Demands advanced by the manifesto included abolition

81 Vesting Property rights directly in the *ryot* or cultivator. Francine R. Frankel, *India's Political Economy…, 32.*

82 Ibid.

83 Francine R. Frankel, *India's Political Economy…*, 55. Kisan Sabhas were sprang up indifferent places eventually formed a national organization named All-India Kisan Sabha (AIKS).

of all zamindari tenures without compensation, abolition of all debts, redistribution of cultivable waste land vesting in government to subsistence farmers and landless farmers..."[84]

The left-wing of the congress party supported the *Kisan Manifesto.* Nehru supported the activities of AIKS, and placed the demand of AIKS at forefront though he was opposed by the conservative majority within the congress party. But the piecemeal approach of congress party towards the demand of AIKS resulted in a wide gap between both.

Soon after the independence, under the leadership of Nehru, the Land Reform Act was implemented, which was a precondition for our economic development. Land is the primary source of livelihood in rural areas. Since inequality in the distribution of the land is the basic cause of economic disparities and privileges, land reform aimed at a more equitable distribution of land so it became an integral part of agrarian reform[85]. D. Bandyopadhyay says [86]"It involves sharing and, in a sense, some transfer of economic (and, with it, political) power from the established landowning class to the rural poor, namely marginal farmers, agricultural workers, and small unsecured tenants of various types."

2.3.1.1. Implementation of the Policy and its failures

In the first five year plan, Land Reform was introduced. The main elements are abolition of intermediaries: tenancy reform comprising regulation of rent, security of tenure, and conferment of ownership rights on tenants; ceiling on landholding and distribution of surplus land; consolidation of holdings; and compilation and updating of land records. There is general agreement that out of these five items, the abolition of intermediaries has been carried out successfully throughout India. There is equally strong general agreement that in

---

84 Francine R. Frankel, *India's Political Economy...*, 56. Kisan Sabhas were sprang up indifferent places eventually formed a national organization named All-India Kisan Sabha (AIKS).

85 Ibid.

86 D. Bandyopadhyay, "Reflections on Land reforms in India Since Independence", in *Industry and Agricuture in India Since Independence Vol. 2*, ed. by. T. V. Sathyamurthy (Delhi: Oxford University Press, 1998), 302.

all other respects very little has been accomplished and much remains to be done.[87] The major outcomes of Land Reform are:

- As the law removed intermediaries, Indian agriculture started moving from semi-feudalism to capitalist relationships. But the capitalistic nature which is superimposed on the semi-feudalistic traditional society carried on the same characteristics of caste and other problems. The rural workers who are mainly Agricultural Labourers and Small Farmers continued to suffer after the implementation of this system.[88]
- Though landlordism is removed by the law, studies show that concealed tenancies of various types are prevalent in many parts of the country.[89]
- Though, for the implementation of Land Reform the rich tenants and Agricultural Labourers fought together against the zamindars, but in the later stage, the new class of peasants who mostly belonged to the rich class of tenants stood against the further distribution of land through radical land reform; this works against the interest of the rural poor, who are mostly Agricultural Labourers.[90]
- It is quite possible that good number of poor tenants lost their rights because they could not challenge their

87 Paramjit S. Judge, *Social Change Through Land Reforms* (New Delhi: Rawat Pub.,1999), 13.; J. Lawrence, *An Ethical Critical of Land reform: with Special Reference to the Kerala Land Reform* (Amendment) Act, 1969 (New Delhi: ISPCK, 1998), 28; D. Bandyopadhyay, op. cit., 303; M. P. Gurusamy, "Land Ceiling Acts and Absentee Landlordism", in *Land Reforms in India, Vol. 9: Tamil Nadu: An Unfinished Task,* ed. by, M. Thangaraj (New Delhi: Sage Pub., 2003), 47.

88 P. C. Joshi, *Land Reforms in India: Trends and Perspectives* (New Delhi: Allied Pub., 1975), 103-104.

89 Ibid.; V. M Rao, "Land Reform Experiences: Perspectives for Strategy and Programmes," *Economic and Political Weekly* 27/26 (June 27, 1992): A 51.

90 J. Lawrence, *An Ethical Critical of Land reform: with Special Reference to the Kerala Land Reform (Amendment) Act, 1969*, 27; Baldev Raj Nayar, op. cit., 179.

landlords. They were pushed into the category of landless agriculture labourers.[91]

- When the ceiling idea was mooted, it was calculated that 35 million hectares of agriculture land would be available for redistribution among the landless and poor peasantry (small farmers). But the surplus land for redistribution has since eroded at a fast pace. At the same time, according to the National Sample Survey report, land alienation and landless households are increasing at a fast rate.[92]
- In spite of the large scale participation of the Dalit agriculture labourers in the agriculture process of the country, they have very little access to land.[93]
- The problem of *benami* transactions and distribution of *benami pattas* figured prominently on land reform programmes in almost all states except ones like West Bengal, Kerala, Tripura and Karnataka.

By looking at the outcomes, it is clear that although the land reform in general negatively affected the landlords, they continued to be a powerful section through the help of *benamies*.

The assessment prepared by the Department of Rural Development (1988) and Ministry of Agriculture (1988) states that "the chief reason for poor implementation of land reform has been the lack of political will."[94] It was because of the presence of landlords in the ruling party and with their economic influence they could protect their land, and land reform did not serve their purpose. And also the conditions of drought and food scarcity during the mid-sixties, the urgency of attaining self-sufficiency in food production and Green Revolution in the latter half of the sixties contributed to the state of official retreat so far as land reform was concerned.[95]

---

91 Ibid.; D. Bandyopadhyay, op. cit., 322-323.

92 Sanjeeb K. Behera (Ed.), *Dalits and Land Reforms in India* (New Delhi: Indian Social Institute, 1999), 2-4.

93 This report is based on the 1991 census, Ibid., 4-5.

94 V. M. Rao, "Land Reform Experiences: Perspectives for Strategy and Programmes", *Economic and Political Weekly* 27/26 (June 27, 1992): A 51

95 D. Bandyopadhyay, op. cit., 323.

Though there was an effort to distribute land to the poor made by Vinoba Bhave, who led *Bhoodan* movement, it could not make a large impact throughout the country.[96] Besides this, the division within the communist led AIKS caused the emergence of the Naxalites. They embarked upon armed struggle in a few villages in West Bengal, Andhra, Bihar, Uttar Pradesh and Orissa. While their main demand was land redistribution, they did not pursue parliamentary path, but revolutionary one; they opposed the tiny section of the rich farmers. In some places they forcefully occupied the land redistributed.[97]

2.3.1.2. Livelihood of Agricultural Labourers and Small Farmers

What happened to employment and ownership pattern of resources during the land reform?

An official survey of unemployment and underemployment conducted in 1972/73 showed that the numbers of unemployed wage-seeking labourers were approximately twice the size anticipated according to the statistical projections based on 1961 census data.[98] The study also reveals that the chronic unemployment affected as many as one-third of all Agricultural Labourers. The census data also reveals the increase of Agriculture Labourers in number. There are various explanations given by different authors;[99] one of the possible

96 K. R. Nanekar, *Bhoodan and the Landless* (Bombay: Poular Prakashan, 1973), 5ff.

97 See more Sunil Sen, *Peasant Movements in India* (New Delhi: K. P. Bagchi & Company, 1982), 212ff.

98 These data were generated through the pilot intensive Rural Employment Project launched by the Department of Community Development in 1972/73 as part of the government's Crash Scheme for Rural Employment. a survey of unemployment and underemployment was conducted in fifteen selected Blocks to get data representative for the country as a whole. India, Ministry of Agriculture, Department of Community Development, unpublished, Cited in Francine R. Frankel, *India's Political Economy…*, 494-495.

99 Major reasons are proposed by Visaria, Vyas, and Bardhan, they have suggested it may be because of natural increase of population, decline of traditional occupations like artisans and they might have joined with agricultural laborers, the influx of surplus labourers from the small and marginal farmers' household

reasons they suggested is that "eviction of tenancy caused the increase of owner-cultivation with hired labour." As far as the resources are concerned, subsequent National Sample Survey report, in Appendix 3.1, reveals the less impact or the poor implication of land reform.

The National Sample Survey of India, in Appendix 3.1, depicts the pattern of agrarian inequality; in 1953-54 the marginal farmers who comprise 61.24% owned only 6.23% of land, at the same time the large farmers who comprise only 3.60% owned 36.17% of the land. However, even after two decades of implementation of land reform laws there had not been any substantial change in the agrarian scenario. The 1971-72 survey figures show that the marginal farmers who comprise 62.62% owns only 9.76%, at the same time the upper strata of rural hierarchy comprising 10%--(Medium, 7.83%, and Large, 2.12%) owns 53.79% of the land. So, Land Reform did not make any substantial influence on the life of the landless.

Along with this study, studies conducted by Asian Development Bank and an enquiry by International Labour Organization[100] give a picture of the state of livelihood of Small Farmers and Agricultural Labourers. Many had received independent access to resources, at the same time many lost their access to resources and occasionally had access to employment. There was also a study which says the less support service to the people who receive land related negatively.[101]

During this time, the Government introduced Community Development Programmes, which was aimed to mobilize large participation of peasant cultivators in labour-intensive agriculture production. And also state-partnered village cooperatives were created to fortify small farmers with cheap credit facilities and economies of bulk purchase and sale of agricultural commodities. Yet, in the absence of effective implementation of all institutional reforms, it proved that it is impossible to provide attractive incentives to the

and finally above mentioned reason, cited in Manabendu Chattopadhyay, op. cit., 8.

100 See more, P. C. Joshi, *Institutional Aspects of Agricultural Development* (New Delhi: Allied Pub., 1987), 192-200.

101 G. Lawrence Arul Raj, *Land reforms* (Madurai: Diwahar Pub., 2001).

majority of small producers for participation in labor-intensive agricultural production programmes.[102]

2.3.1.3. Analysis of Land Reform Policy in Relation to the Four Units in the Society

In this analysis, an effort has been made to understand the influence of Land Reform policy, which is implemented by the State (s) unit, on the question of livelihood of h-1, h-2, h-3, and h-4 units.

The Land Reform Policy aimed to distribute the ownership of resources to the landless (h-4) in our country; they were traditionally engaged in agriculture work (employment), but had no power to control the resources; not having equitable claim on production, only their labour power can combine with resources of employers (market-oriented farmers).

So, this policy aimed to redistribute the so-called waste land as well as the land of market-oriented farmers, who control more resources. Through this most of the traditional landless labourers (h-4) were supposed to move towards subsistence farmers (h-2) or self-sufficient group (h-1). Their access to resources was the major concern of this policy. The market-oriented farmers (h-3) were also supposed to move towards h-2 section, by allowing the landless to hold control over resources.

State (s) units also tried to extent its activity chains in favour of h-2 section through Community Development Programmes, Labor-Intensive Agricultural Production Programmes, etc., so, the state wants to have link with h-2 section, who were earlier holding no land or little land. Through this linkage the state wants to ensure them livelihood.

This policy aimed to check the activity chain which works in an oppressive way among the household units especially against the landless, and if this activity chain restructures through Land Reform policy then it would help in improving the livelihood of these sections. So, the government introduced this policy. Though policy introduced, as we have discussed above, failed to break the traditional activity chains which works against the h-4 sections. In

102 Francine R. Frankel, *India's Green Revolution...*, 3-4.

brief, Land Reform was implemented primarily for the benefit of Landless Agriculture Labourers (h-4).

But, though Nehru started this policy to make structural changes as a pre-requisite to development, he could not achieve his expectation.

2.3.2. Green Revolution and Livelihood

In the beginning of 1958, slow growth rates in the agriculture sector became a serious limiting factor in the overall rate of economic advance. So, the planning commission announced "a fresh consideration of the assumptions, methods, and techniques as well as the machinery of planning and plan implementation in the field of agriculture"[103] it was a departure from earlier programme. It has nothing to do with institutional reforms, and concentrated on certain area in the beginning.

In brief, we can say, policy emphasis had shifted from institutional to technological factors. Thus, the land use pattern concentrated on commercial rather than subsistence production. The Green Revolution, which is associated with high yield varieties of seeds, ushered in new phase of agricultural upgrades and modernization.

There are reports regarding the influences of Green Revolution on the livelihood of subsistence/small farmers. It was generally agreed that the poor farmers' income was inadequate to buy the necessary components of the high-yield technology---irrigation, high-yield seeds, fertilizers, pesticides etc.[104] It was because the income had stagnated on these farms over the years due to the government's elitist approach by concentrating on the wealthier and progressive farmers under two major schemes, namely, Intensive Agriculture

103 India, Planning Commission, Memorandum on the Fourth-Five Year Plan (Delhi, October 1964), 26, 29, cited in Francine R. Frankel, *India's Green Revolution…*, 5.

104 T. C. Sharma and O. Coutinhao, *Green revolution Gaps: A Geographical Analysis* (Jaipur: Rawat Pub., 1989), 6; also see K. P. Kannan, *Of Rural Proletarian Struggles* (Delhi: Oxford University Press, 1988), 293: John Hariss, *Capitalism and Peasant Farming* (Delhi: Oxford University Press, 1982), 209; Ben Jackson, *Poverty and the Planet: A Question of Survival* (New York: Penguin Books, 1990), 6, 55, 56.

Development Programme (IADP) and the High Yielding Varieties Programme (HYVP), initially pioneered by Ford foundation. The situation has not changed much in spite of the Small Farmers Development Agency (SFDA) Programme and the Drought-Prone Area Programmes (DPAP) launched in 1969-71 to reduce the income disparities.[105]

At the same time, new technology enabled the rich farmers to acquire more and more fertile irrigated land. A survey carried out in Punjab showed that between 1955-56 and 1967-68, the rich farmers, who hold between 100 and 150 acres of land, increased their total landholding mainly through purchase of the small holdings.[106] This fact confirms that a good number of tenants, share croppers, small and poor farmers must have lost their land. Also, the small and marginal farmers generally had to depend on the rich farmers and money lenders for credit at a very high rates of interest. High yield varieties of seed and fertilizers demanded more water; as a result access to water restricted those who cannot afford the cost of deepening their wells regularly. Many of the subsistence farmers did not have facilities for irrigation and were compelled to sell their land.[107] This shows that the Green Revolution had a negative influence on the livelihood of small farmers.[108]

The influence of green revolution on Agricultural Labourers can also be seen in various reports and studies. R. S. Sidhu, and Sukhpal Singh, in their study, showed the reduction of labour in agriculture. The main reason for this was the introduction of combine harvesters

---

105 Report on the Intensive Agricultural District Program (1960-68), Vol. I, 12, cited in Francine R. Frankel, *India's Green Revolution…*, 9; Appu. P. S, "Agrarian Structure and Rural Development," *Economic and Political Weekly* 9/39 (September 28, 1974): A 70-75.

106 Asok Rudra, A. Majid and B. D. Talib, "Big Farmers of Punjab" *Economic and Political Weekly* (27 Sept., 1969) quoted in J. Lawrence, op. cit., 27.

107 Nicholas Hildyard, "Too Many for What?," *The Ecologist Asia* 5/3 (May/June, 1997): 24; also see Francine R. Frankel, *India's Green Revolution…*, 39; and, Bharat Dogra, *Empty Stomachs and Packed Godowns* (New Delhi: BDPub.,1987), 85-86.

108 How it systematically deprives the condition of the poor farmers has explained American Political scientist: Susan George, *Food for Beginners* (London: Writers and Readers Pub., 1982), 134ff.

on a large scale for harvesting and threshing operations in wheat and paddy.[109]

This study shows the fact that the introduction of modern production technology for wheat and rice made change in the demand for field agricultural employment. There was a study conducted by the Comprehensive Scheme to Study Cost of Cultivation of Principal Crops in Punjab, which reports on the use of human labour in wheat production; for one hectare of land 25.73% human Labour decreased in between the years 1985-88 to 1998-2000. Same picture can be seen in the paddy crop. For one hectare of land 47.28% of human labour decreased in between the years 1981-1983 to 1998-99.[110] This study shows that the Green Revolution had a negative influence on landless Agricultural Labourers. They lost employment, which was essential to them; traditional know-how had been replaced with new technology. There are also studies that confirmed that the Green Revolution negatively affected female cultivators and female agriculture labourers.[111] However, Frankel says, in the initial stage of Green Revolution, Agricultural Labourers had advantage though it had deteriorated when mechanization increased.[112]

---

109 R. S. Sidhu, and Sukhpal Singh, "Agricultural Wages and Employment," *Economic and Political Weekly* 39/37 (September, 2004): 4132- 4133.

110 Cited in, Ibid; also see K.P. Kannan, op. cit., 293; Amarjit Chandan, "Victims of Green Revolution," *Economic and Political Weekly* 14/25 (June 23, 1979); 1035.

111 Maria Mies, "Capitalist Development and Subsistence Production: Rural woman in India", in *Women: the Last Colony,* ed. by Maria Mies (New Delhi: Kali for Women, 1988), 27-45.; also see Vandhana Shiva, *Staying Alive: Women, Ecology and Survival in India* (New Delhi: Kali for Women, 1988), 96ff.

112 Francine R. Frankel, *India's Green Revolution…*, 38-39. Present Prime Minister gave a call for 'second Green Revolution' (Gene Revolution), and stated that the first Green Revolution ran out of steam for two reasons---it did not benefit dry land farming, and was not scale-neutral and had thus only benefited large farms and big farmers. He claimed that Second Green Revolution would concentrate mainly on marginal and small farmers. Ruddar Dutt, "Second Green Revolution," *Janata* 61/23 (July 16, 2006): 4-5; However, Vandhana Shiva observes that "the second Green Revolution based on biotechnology and genetic engineering will have even higher social and environmental costs than the first Green Revolution." Vandana Shiva, "From Seed to Retail: Globalization Creates Monopolies in Agriculture," *Janata* 61/15 (May 21, 2006): 6.

2.3.2.1. Analysis of Green Revolution Policy in Relation to the Four Units in the Society

In this analysis, researcher tries to understand Green Revolution policy's influence on the activity chain of these four units.

The above discussion shows that, if h-2 and h-1 units (small/marginal farmers) want to have an access to the benefit of this policy, they need link with market, which is now national and global. It is possible only through the help of local money lender or 'b' (bank). All the technological assistance they get in the market is highly expensive and need of water also depend on investment. It is beyond their reach. So, either they depend on the h-3 unit (rich farmer) or most of the h-2 section sell their land and move to become h-4 (Agriculture labour) unit. But, in the h-4 unit many lose their employment in the agriculture sector because most of the manual work is now done by machine, so the h-4 section has moved from skilled to unskilled or underemployment.

So, this policy mainly aimed to increase the production. And it benefitted mainly the h-3 unit, f (enterprise/corporate), and b (bank) units. It had adverse influence on the livelihood of h-2 and h-4 units. And also there will be long term adverse influence on nature.

2.3.3. Contract Farming and Livelihood

In the post reform period, policy emphasis has shifted to liberalizing trade in agriculture. With the establishment of WTO on January 1, 1995 and India becoming a member, all 'Qualitative Restrictions' were dismantled by the end of March 2001. The expectation is that, this policy shift would provide an opportunity for our farmers and agro-based industries to get into the world markets. And it is necessary to remove legal restrictions on the lease market for agricultural land as well as to facilitate growth of operational holdings of small farmers.[113]

The farms are integrated into agro-processing companies, which has extended technical expertise and financial support to the farmers to grow high value-added crops. However, farmers have lost

113 R. Radakrishna, "Agriculture Growth, employment and Poverty: A Policy Perspective", *Economic and Political Weekly* 37/3 (January 19-25, 2002): 245.

their right to choose seeds, thus undermining their relationship to production;[114] they are allowed to cultivate only the seeds which the agro-processing company chooses and also are required to sell their production to the company, which decides the price. Over a long period, as farmers lose their touch with traditional knowledge on cultivation, they may be reduced into mere instruments in the hand of these multinationals. Vandhana Shiva states that contract farming "has already eliminated the small farmers and replaced the sustainable agriculture by capital-intensive agro businesses, based on internal output like pesticides, fertilizers and genetic engineering",[115] and "(the) farmers are transformed from producers to consumers of corporate patented agriculture products,...and the global economy becomes a means for the rich to rob the poor of their right to food and their right to life."[116] Thus, this policy changes the use pattern of resources, thereby it promotes export production at the cost of local food security.

2.3.3.1. Analysis of Contract Farming in Relation to the three Units in the Society

In this analysis, researcher tries to understand influence of contract farming on the activity chain of three units.

The contract farming has been introduced in the places where green revolution implemented. Through this policy, h-2, sections, who were mostly concentrated on their own need or subsistence economy, are now producing for the global market. And also h-2 and h-3 relates with corporate (f-unit), who decides what to produce and invests capital intensive technologies. The role of h-4 sections is very minimal because new capital intensive technologies replace the labour intensive technologies. The means of production, i.e., land and water became subject to exhaustive technologies.

114 Vandana Shiva, "New Zamindari and Undermining of food Security in India," *Third World Resurgence* 53/54 (January-February, 1995): 7-8.

115 Vandhana Shiva, "South Safeguards Farmers Rights: On Agricultural Biodiversity," *The Ecologist Asia* 5/3 (May-June, 1997): 6.

116 Vandana shiva, *Stolen Harvest: The Hijacking of the Global Food Supply* (London: Zed Book, 2000), 7. See more Piyush, "Contract Farming in India: Death Knell for Farmers", *Lok Samvad* (Sept., 2003): 16.

In brief, among the above discussed policies, land reform is to make institutional changes, mainly aimed to change the ownership pattern of land resources, which is the major source of livelihood. But the lack of implementation causes the condition of the landless to remain the same. The second policy mainly aimed to increase the agriculture production, but nothing to do with its distribution. It is mainly for a pro-market oriented farmer as well as pro- major firms; which produce high yield seeds and technologies such as tractors, harvesters and other machines. And the third policy is mainly aimed to benefit 'f 'unit (Corporates), and also on the one side, initially the h-3 section may get 'capital', but on the other side they may lose the means of production, i.e., land and due to the over use of ground water and chemicals they may get deprived of it later.

2.4. How SEZ Differs from Earlier Land Related Policies?

2.4.1. Land Reform and Special Economic Zone

The main slogan of Land Reform was "Land to the Tiller".[117] On the contrary, the SEZ can be called as Land Deform Policy, the prime purpose of the land changes; it deforms the land, by establishing industry. If the slogan of land reform policy was "the land to the tiller", the slogan of SEZ can be called "the land from the tiller." Land reform policy was mainly concentrated on the redistribution to the tillers--collecting the land from the landlords and redistributing--but the SEZ is aimed at collecting the pieces of land from the farmers and giving them to the big co-operatives, i.e., shift to large units.

2.4.2. Green Revolution and Special Economic Zone

A decade later land reform agenda was pushed into background and Green Revolution arrived in the forefront. Though, Green Revolution had adverse impact on the peasantry differentiation, i.e., poor farmer became poorer and rich became richer, soil degradation, and created inequality between regions,[118] it did not take away land from agriculture production rather it mainly aimed to increase

117 Quoted by C. T. Kurian, *Global Capitalism and Indian Economy* (Delhi: Orient Longman, 1994), 34.

118 C. T. Kurian, *The Economy...*, 306-307.

the food production of our country and to have self sufficiency in food production. To implement this policy government provided subsidies and other related help to the land owners mainly to the rich farmers.

On the contrary, SEZ takes and shifts the use of land from agriculture production to industrial production, mainly to increase export-oriented production. The government has given subsidies and other related benefits to the big business houses and the land has been taken away from the farmers both the rich and small.

2.4.3. Contract Farming and Special Economic Zone

As part of globalization and related policies, the government withdrew from its welfare approach, and allowed the transnational agro-food corporations to enter Indian agriculture. Under the new definition of 'land Reform'[119] there is an increasing pressure to allow companies to undertake direct farm production especially in the areas of horticulture, floriculture, and agro-forestry. The design is to alter the land use pattern geared to their profit interests.[120]

Under the contract farming, the farmers are commissioned to produce and supply specific product, in specific quantities and of specific quality at a specified time and at a specified price. The company provides seeds, fertilizers, technology, credit and also farm equipments. However, Contract farming is confined to few areas and few products.[121]

Here, we can see the gradual transition of policy that now moves land into the hands of big cooperatives that play the role of farmers

119 In India, the corporate sector has been prevented from entering direct farm production because of the land ceiling laws. The low ceiling limits do not allow scale intensive farming in which companies are interested. Only the plantation sector exempted from the land ceiling regulations. But today, there is an increasing pressure to allow companies to undertake direct farm production especially in the areas of horticulture, floriculture and agro-forestry. The demand is to substantially extend the land ceiling or remove it together. See more Jaya Mehta, *Changing Agrarian Structure in Indian Economy*, 14-15.

120 Ibid., 15-16.

121 Tomoto crop in Punjab (HLL, Pepsi and Nijjar), Mustard crop in Punjab (Markfed, a para-statal cooperative body), potatoes (Mcdonalds) etc., are some of the examples. Ibid.

and even forgetting the role of rich farmers who were mostly the landlords previously, who were at least playing a major role earlier. At the same time, they use the land for the agriculture production, though it leads to degradation of land as it was in Green Revolution. In SEZ, big cooperatives primarily get the ownership of the land and the major difference is that they change from agriculture production to industrial production.

Conclusion

The adverse influence on the question of livelihood of Small Farmers and Agriculture Labourers has intensified in each policy. Though there was an effort from the Nehruvian Government soon after the independence to change the institutional framework so that the livelihood question might be addressed, the failure of implementation of Land Reform could not make expected change in the question of livelihood of these communities. Then Green Revolution and later contract farming did not address the question of livelihood rather it intensified the livelihood problems of these communities, though total food production of the nation had increased.

The ongoing onslaught on the question of livelihood of Small Farmers and Agriculture Labourers continue with the new policies of the government, including SEZ. This is discussed in detail in the following chapter.

Chapter III

SEZ and the Question of Livelihood

Introduction

The question of livelihood has been challenged by various factors. Though many of the earlier policies aimed to promote livelihood or standard of life it never reached the bottom of society. As we have discussed in previous chapter either it reaches among the middle class or just the dominant class of the society. Today, when the government moved towards a development model which validates export growth more than employment and social security, it has adverse influence on the livelihood of people specially the Small Farmers and Agriculture Labourers. Opposition to the policies of the government especially against SEZ highlights the livelihood challenges of Agriculture community. This chapter explains the influence of SEZ on the livelihood of Agriculture Labourers and Small Farmers, which is based on the researcher's empirical findings.

3.1. SEZ and Question of Livelihood of Affected People

Against SEZs, massive strikes and protest are going on in different places in order to protect the livelihood base, i.e., Land and Water, of the rural population in the country.[122] The farming communities, Tribals, Dalits and Adivasis are in forefront of these strikes. Their main aim is to protect their land. Most of the agriculture land has been acquired for this purpose. At the same time, the main leaders of ruling class repeatedly emphasis that only the waste land will be used for SEZ. But, land classification in India is a complex issue.

So, the threat of livelihood is very visible. It is mainly because of forcible transfer of the small & private and corporate ownership of the resources of the common people to the hands of big companies.

The tendency of this problem is evident in the following empirical study of the researcher.

---

122 In Haryana, near Gurgan land allocated for reliance as part of SEZ, where 50% of the village population depends on agriculture for their livelihood. For them, no compensation, and not getting any employment-only for the families who give up their land for project will be given employment; T. K. Rajalaksmi, "Brave New World of Tax exemptions," *Frontline* 23/13 (July 1-14, 2006): 35.

In Maharastra, at Raigad district villagers are fighting against SEZ it is to protect their resources; land, which is cultivable and water is available from Hetwana dam. And also fishermen who live in this area now face threat of their livelihood. Dionne Bunsha, "Rural Resistance: Gearing up for the Battle," *Frontline* 23/20 (October 7-20, 2006): 9-10

The farmers of Kanzhawala village in north east Delhi and nearby villages had been on an indefinite *Dharna* demanding the return of their land that has been acquired by the Delhi government. It says that two thousand Agricultural Labourers are currently living in this village who depend solely agriculture for their livelihood "Peasant Struggle against Forcible Land Acquisition," *People's Voice* 30/19 (October 1-15, 2008): 8.

Besides there are many places like Nandigram, Noida, Madurai, Manglore and so on people's resistance against SEZ in order to protect their resources from forced acquirement.

3.2. Question of Livelihood of Agricultural Labourers and Small farmers: A Field Study

3.2.1. The Study Design and Procedures

3.2.1.1. Objective of the Study

- The main objective of this study is to know the influence and possible influence of SEZ on livelihood.
- To know the livelihood condition of Agriculture Labourers and Small Farmers.

The main questions which are going to be discussed here are: What happened to the access to resources? Which are mainly land, water and livestock in the selected areas, before and after setting up SEZ. And also, What is the condition of employment (Skill, Wage, time, number of working days) before and after setting up of SEZ, and What is the possible threat to employment?

3.2.1.2. Method of Sampling

Place: The Researcher has selected two SEZ areas for the study. One is at Moradabad SEZ in Uttar Pradesh, which is located in the Northern part of India. In this place, Land has acquired from the villagers and wall has been set up. It has planned to use at the first phase for sector specific SEZ. It covers four villages, namely, Karanpur, Lalpur Gangawari, Kondari, and Bahadarpur Rajput.

The Second area is at Kallikudi area in Thirumangalam Block in Madurai District, Tamil Nadu, which is located in Southern part of India. The particular village (Panchayat) in which the researcher has concentrated the study is Sivarikottai. In this place, land is marked for setting up SEZ.

3.2.1.3. Sample Units

Agriculture Labourers (AL, h-4): Agricultures Labourers are the people who do not own agriculture land or keep small piece of land, and mainly work in the land of others for daily wages.

Small farmers/subsistence farmers (SF, h-2): Small Farmers, who use primarily family labour in their field. They produce for their needs.

Market-oriented Farmers (MF, h-3): Market-oriented Farmers who mainly produce for selling in the market, and use employees for the work in the field.

Number of people for interview selected from each category in Moradabad SEZ area is not based on the exact percentage of population but it was based on the information received from the Villagers and Block Development Officer. As per the information, majority among the villagers are small/subsistence farmers, then Agriculture labourers and small group of Market oriented farmers. So subsistence/small farmers have selected larger number (9 samples) than Agriculture Labourers and Market Oriented Farmers, and Agriculture Labourers selected (7 samples) are more than Market-oriented Farmers (4 samples). In Madurai SEZ, number of people selected for interview are equal in number.

Each unit category has again divided into different caste groups- however, though Muslim community has divided within themselves into different castes, the researcher has taken them as one community because they prefer to identify themselves as Muslims and many hesitated to reveal their particular caste identity. Each unit categories has mainly been selected from the major/dominant caste group in the selected area of study. In the Moradabad SEZ area, the researcher has selected household unit, each household includes father and mother and three or two sons and their children. In Madurai the researcher, selected sample from male ownership household and female ownership households, which generally include father, mother and children.

Officials: Assistant Development Commissioner of Moradabad SEZ, Village Chief/President, belongs to Bahujan Samajwadi Party (BSP), Block Development Officer and Politician, belongs to Samajwadi Party (SP) are selected for interview.

3.2.1.4. Method of Data Collection

To collect necessary information, the researcher has prepared different questionnaires for two selected places. Questionnaires for Moradabad SEZ area are divided into three sections:

The first section is to know process and procedures of the SEZ; nature of land, size of the land, how did developers acquire the land? Regarding compensation, what promises were given to the villagers before occupying the land?

The second section is to know the condition of livelihood; it has divided into two sections: one is to know the condition of resources before and after setting up the zone, and second is to know the condition of wage, skill, and number of employment days before and after setting up the zone.

The third section also is to know the condition of livelihood mainly by comparing (before and after setting up zone) the cost of living in relation to the basic necessities of life.

In Madurai, SEZ questionnaires are prepared to know two kinds of answers:

Firstly, to know the basic information about the land at Sivarikottai.

Secondly, to know the situation regarding existing livelihood condition and assess the possible threat to their livelihood.

3.2.1.5. Framework of field study Analysis

Field study Analysis is based on the Descriptive Method of C.T. Kurian.[123] In this analysis, the Researcher makes an attempt to explain the role of these three units (h-2, Subsistence Farmers, h-3, Market Oriented Farmers, and h-4, Agriculture Labourers) on these three basic functions of economy (exercise control over resources, combine resource and labour in production and decide on the claims of members on the produce).

How these functions work out before and after the implementation of SEZ in relation to their livelihood?

3.2.2. Moradabad Special Economic Zone

Western Uttar Pradesh is a fertile land blessed with two great rivers, Ganges and Yamuna, on its two sides. It is one of the most important food production areas. Due to the high fertility of the land major

123 It has explained in Chapter II in detail.

proportion of its population depend on agriculture for livelihood. Moradabad is one of the important city in western Uttar Pradesh. This place is known as Brass City of India, and it is also one of the leading export cities in India. As it is already a leading export city, the Government of India aimed to expand its export-oriented production as part of economic reform. So, in 2003 as part of the Exim policy central government selected a place for SEZ in Moradabad. This SEZ is a joint venture of both state and central government.

The Researcher in his study visited and spent a brief period (30 days) in these four villages and collected 20 (household) samples of affected people under three categories: Agricultural Labourers, Small Farmers, and Market-oriented Farmers. The researcher has divided each category into groups: Hindu Takhur (HT), Hindu Jatavs (HJ), and Muslim community (MC).

3.2.2.1. Process and procedure of SEZ in Moradabad

The researcher has done field study to know the process and procedures of setting up SEZ at Moradabad. To know this, the researcher has asked two questions: Size and nature of land, and attitude of officials. This again is divided into four areas: regarding information, process of acquisition, compensation and promises, and negotiation.

3.2.2.1.1. Size and Nature of Land acquired for SEZ

The researcher's finding in relation to the size and nature of the land acquired for SEZ is that the size of the land acquired in this area is 421.565 acres consisting of four main villages, to which all the samples of affected people (20 persons), and interviewed people (4 persons) agreed.

Regarding the nature of the land, all of them agreed that it was totally private land, which was owned by villagers and used only for cultivation in all seasons (three cultivation in a year). However, Assistant Development Commissioner stated that it was a surplus land, i.e., villagers were keeping more land.[124] But, the research reveals that this claim is not correct. Most of the villagers have small areas of land for their livelihood.

---

124 Interview with Alok Pandey, Assistant Development Commissioner, SEZ Moradabad, 5th May, 2008.

In this place residential land was avoided from the acquirement. Because of that no displacement has occurred. But, it was reported in the local Newspaper, *Dainik Jagarun* that SEZ of Moradabad will be expanding further, that may cause displacement.

3.2.2.1.2. Attitude of officials

3.2.2.1.3. Proper information or Vague Information

The researcher conducted a study to find out whether villagers were given proper information before acquiring the land or not? The study shows that, in Appendix 3.12, among the selected samples most of them, i.e., 87.50% agreed that land was acquired through vague information; there was no information given to the villagers (all the Small Farmers and Agriculture Labourers agreed to this fact); they heard about the land acquisition through village chief but it was ambiguous; They did not know that whose land was going to be acquired and for what purpose it was going to be acquired? However, 8.34% (Market–Oriented rich Farmers and Assistant Development Commissioner) agreed that it was through proper information. Information was passed to the villagers by the officials of UPSIDC regarding the size of the land, and the mapping of the area. And 4.17% did not know about it, he was a block official.[125]

The researcher's finding on the time span given to the villagers before acquiring the land shows that, land was acquired one year after vague or proper information.

3.2.2.1.4. How did UPSIDC acquire the Land either through Force or Persuasion?

The researcher's findings show that, 91.66% (22 persons) agree that land was acquired through force. 4.17% (1 person) agree that it was through persuasion, and 4.17% (1 person) did not know about it. Aneez Ahamad, village *pradhan* (chief) of Kondari, said that "when land acquisition started, the villagers organized rally and peacefully moved towards the officers, who came to mark the land. The police who accompanied the officials arrested the villagers, who were

---

125 Interview with Anurag Bhatnagar, Block Officer, Kundarki Block, Kunderki Block, Moradabad, 15th May, 2008.

protesting peacefully against the forceful land acquisition, and as a result twenty-five people were charged FIR by Moradabad police, and still the villagers have to go to station to sign and still case is pending."[126]

3.2.2.1.5. Compensation and Promises

Regarding the compensation, the researcher's findings show that, 95.83% (23 persons) agreed that UPSIDC has offered Rs. 50,000/- per *biga* (6 cent), and 4.17% (1 person) do not know how much was the compensation. Among the selected samples, 79.1% (19 persons) agree the compensation is less than the market price of the land, 16.68% (4 persons) agree that it was equal with market value, and 4.17% (I person) does not know about it.

Among the people who lost land 88.88% (16 persons) received compensation, 11.12% (2 persons) did not receive compensation, because they demanded more money and argued that Rs. 50,000 per *biga* (6 cent) is less than the market value. Hence, they filed case against UPSIDC, and they are not ready to accept the compensation.[127] Assistant Development Commissioner agrees that people received compensation, except the few who filed case against UPSIDC,[128] and block official does not know about the compensation.[129]

Regarding the promise of UPSIDC, the Researcher's findings show that, 4.17% acknowledge that no promises were given by UPSIDC, 4.17% do not know whether promises are given or not, and 91.66% agree that promises were given by UPSIDC. The Promises are:

- All the village roads will be maintained in good condition.

---

126 Interview with Aneez Ahmad, Village Chief, Kondari village, Kunderki Block, Moradabad, 7th May, 2008.

127 Interview with Bilal Ahamd, Market-oriented Farmer, Bahadarpur.Village, Kunderki Block, Moradabad, 10th May, 2008.

128 Interview with Alok Pandey, Assistant Development Commissioner, SEZ Moradabad, 5th May, 2008.

129 Anurag Bhatnagar, Block Official, kunderki Block, Mroradabad, 15th May, 2008.

- Jobs will be given to the villagers. Only those who lose one acre will be eligible for job (one Acre/ one Person job).
- Latrine will be built for each household
- Electricity will be provided for the villagers who do not have connection and fixing the street lights in the village area.
- Hospital will be set up.

The research findings show that 91.66% (22 persons) agreed UPSIDC did not fulfill any of these promises, 4.17% (1 person) agree that no promises were given to the villagers so no point in fulfilling it. 4.17% (1 person) do not know about it.

3.2.2.1.6. Who Negotiated on behalf of villagers?

The research findings show that, 87.50% (20 persons) agree that the villagers raised their demand through village chiefs, and other political leaders, but UPSIDC officials only finalized it. 8.34% agree that rich farmers negotiated. 4.17% (1 person) agree that village leaders like *Pradhan* (village chief), and local political leaders, negotiated with UPSIDC.

3.2.2.2. Condition of Livelihood

The study shows the influence on livelihood of agriculture labourers and small farmers. The researcher has focused the main theme 'livelihood' in relation to access to resources; land, water, and livestock, and also condition of employment.

3.2.2.2.1. Condition of Resources of Agricultural Labourers and Small Farmers

The main resources of farming community are land, water, and livestock. The land acquirement for SEZ resulted in acquiring their resources. The resources are the prime source of the livelihood of this community. So, the question of livelihood is based on the influence of SEZ, it can be assessed by asking, How the access of villagers to resources is affected after setting up the SEZ?

The researcher's findings, in Appendix 3.2, suggest a trend. It indicates adverse influence on the non-labour resources of Small

Farmers and Agriculture Labourers after setting up the SEZ. It shows 95% (19 persons) have suffered a negative influence on their land and related income. Before setting up SEZ they were holding more land than after setting up the SEZ. Though they were given compensation they were not able to purchase the same size of land with the compensation. It is because market price is high. Though few market-oriented farmers were able to purchase land with the compensation, but is away from their village. So they have to suffer more expense for travel and cultivation. And for some, family labour is not possible as it is away from their village.

5% (1 person) has experienced no change, one market-oriented farmer able to purchase same amount of land in another village, where they have already landholdings.

Among the samples no one has felt positive impact; with the compensation they could not get more land than their holdings before setting up SEZ.

Regarding the water resources, 80% (16 persons) of them have been disadvantaged on the condition of water. Among the farmers those who purchased land with the compensation money get water from deeper than on the land which they were holding before setting up SEZ. They depend on ground water for the cultivation.

Among the samples 20% (4 persons) have no change, because they were not able to purchase land with the money. As they are not displaced from the village they can use their own bore well for their daily needs.

Among the samples no one has positive impact. No one get water from a well shallower than the one on holding which is acquired for SEZ.

And finally, condition of the income from the livestock shows that 55% (11 persons) have been disadvantaged. The villagers depend on land for the cattle grazing. When the land was acquired for SEZ, the expenses for keeping livestock increased creating a further burden on their income from the livestock. And some have sold livestock and kept only few. The Small Farmers are the most affected section.

45% (9 persons) have no change; among them two are market-oriented farmers. They were able to get fodder from their own land holdings in nearby villages. And others are able to keep now same number of livestock as before.

Among the samples no one has benefited. No one could purchase more livestock nor they were able to reduce expenses for keeping livestock.

3.2.2.2.2. Condition of Employment (Wage, Skill, and Employment days)

The researcher's findings related to the condition of labour resources was mainly divided into three areas; level of wage, employment days, use of personal skills. The researcher's findings are based on a question: What is the condition of employment (Wage, Skill, and employment days) after setting up SEZ?

The researcher's findings, in Appendix 3.3, indicate that, 85% (17 persons) get less income after setting up SEZ. Before setting up SEZ, most of them were generally engaged in agriculture work in their own field or others field, earlier only some Agricultural Labourers used to go for non-agriculture employment in the city. They work as contract labourers for more time and had less wage than agriculture work, Rs. 60 for contract laborers Rs. 80 or 90 for agriculture work. But, in harvesting seasons, agriculture labourers get share of production, instead of wage. That is enough for one year for a four member family.[130] After setting up SEZ, many go to city or other villages, where they do not get regular work and expenses also increase due to travel, food, etc. Finally, in a month comparatively they get now lesser wage than earlier. Market-oriented Farmers who were working in their own field now find it difficult to go and work in far places, so they prefer to give the land for lease which they have purchased in another village.

15% (3 persons) do not have any change. These are market-oriented farmers, who work in their own field, which have not come into the SEZ area. And the land they purchased is maintained by agriculture laborers of another village.

No one has increased wages after setting up the SEZ. Though apparently some (causal labour) get more wages outside, although

130 Sasikala, Agriculture Labour, Moradabad, 17 May 2008.

the expenses have also increased. Few go for drilling bore well. But, after spending for travel and food no or less income is left for their benefit.

Regarding the condition of labour skill, 85% (17 persons) moved towards unskilled labour. Traditionally, all of them were working as agriculture labourers so, they all were skilled in working on the field. They do not need any instructor or supervisor over them. They were well aware about their work. Their skill also relates to family labour. But now they are not able to do it. Now those who go for work in city are new to their work. Many are going to small export processing units, where they are supervised and instructed. As they are not skilled they are not paid regularly and their duties keep on changing. Women were mostly affected compared to men in the work field. Women have to work with men in the city with poor sanitation and unhygienic basic amenities. Some are not able to travel long distance for new job because they have to look after their children and take-care of livestock.

15% (3 persons) did not have any change, these are from market-oriented farmers who are able to purchase and also work with their land in nearby villages. And no one had moved towards an employment with better skilled labour.

Regarding the condition of the employment days there are 75% (15 persons) who have fewer employment days. It is because they were not having regular work in the cities, where they are contract labourers. Earlier they were able to work in the Agriculture field at the same time some go as contract labourers. Now mostly they have to depend on contract labour which is not regular.

25% (5 persons) don't have any change among them, most of them are market-oriented farmers and one household of agriculture labourer left to nearby village, where their relative lives, so they were able to get same employment days.

3.2.2.2.3. Condition of the Cost of Living

Apart from the condition of both resources and employment, the researcher has studied the cost of living of villagers after setting up SEZ. It is mainly in relation to the education of children in the village, and the condition of housing, health, food habits and sources of food items.

3.2.2.2.4. Condition of Housing

The Researcher has studied the condition of housing after setting up the SEZ: positive influence; good housing condition, negative influence; bad housing condition or more rent, and no change in their housing condition.

The research findings, in Appendix 3.4, show that, there is no change in the housing condition of the people; it shows there is no direct displacement in this place.

3.2.2.2.5. Condition of Education

The researcher has studied the situation regarding the education after setting up the SEZ in three areas: change of school, change in distance between home and school and change in school fee and transport expenses.

The researcher's findings, in Appendix 3.5 show that, there is no change in the school, distance between school and home and only 5% (1 person) had negative impact. Regarding the fee and transportation expenses only 5% (1 person) had negative impact. It is because one of the way which was used by the villagers is now closed by the wall of SEZ, so the household has to use transport to send children to get school bus. Generally there is no change in the education situation. For setting up Moradabad SEZ, no school infrastructure has been removed and no displacement has been occurred in the first phase of SEZ in this area.

3.2.2.2.6. Condition of Health

The researcher has studied health conditions in relation to villagers' access to hospital /clinic, and their health condition after setting up SEZ.

The researcher's findings, in Appendix 3.6, show that, there is no change in access to hospital/clinic mainly because there is no hospital/clinic available in the village, and the same was available only in the Block centre. Regarding the health condition, it shows that, 65% (13 persons) say there is no change in their health condition before and after setting up the SEZ. 35% (7 persons) were not aware about the health problems if any. This shows health conditions and access to hospital have not made completely negative impact till now.

3.2.2.2.7. Condition of Food Habits and Source of Food Items

The researcher has studied the pattern of food habits and source of food items in relation to its change; either positive or negative, or no change.

The researcher's findings, in Appendix 3.7, show the trend of the pattern of food habits. It indicates negative influence for 40% (8 persons) of the people; among the samples all of them are agriculture Labourers and small farmers, they mainly depend on their fields. They received the share of grains and pulses as wage during the harvesting time. But, when they lost the access to resources and employment (Agriculture), their access to the sources to the food also changed from the village field to market, and in the market comparatively they have to pay more. So, their food habit also forced to change. And also many were not able to sustain their livestock as they lost land, it resulted the increase in cost of living.

60% (12 persons) of them do not have any change most of them are market-oriented farmers, and others able to manage though income is comparatively less. After setting up SEZ no one claimed that they have improved their food habits.

Regarding the source of food 75% (15 persons) have experienced a negative influence, they depend more on market, which is flexible and costs them more. Earlier they were mainly dependent on subsistence economy.

25% (5 persons) don't experience any change, still they have some holdings and most of them are market-oriented farmers. And some others have land for their needs and they depend on them.

And no one has benefited from the change.

3.2.2.3. Analysis of field findings of SEZ in Moradabad

The fertile nature of land dictates the internal activity of the units' (h-2, h-4, and h-3) dependency on the land resources. The disruption on this activity chains is because of the forceful acquirement of land resources. The compensation given for resources is less; and not in proportion to the market price. Compensation was received by only those who had access to resources through ownership and not for the people who had access resources through labour. Even among the Subsistence/Small Farmers, few were not able to use the amount which they received as compensation meaningfully.[131] This jeopardized the future of the family. The promises for the basic needs along with compensation were not fulfilled. Negotiation was made by the *pradans,* who were mainly h-3 sections. However, one *pradhan* did not receive compensation.

This analysis looks, before and after setting up SEZ, at the activity chains in which these units (h-2, h-3, and h-4) function, and their involvement in the three basic functions of an economy are: exercise control over resources, combine resources and labour in production and they decide on the claims of members on the produce. It mainly focuses on how the change of involvement influences the livelihood of these sections.

After the implementation of SEZ, majority agree that the size of land they could purchase was smaller in comparison to the land they had before SEZ.[132] Among them most of them are from h-2 (Small Farmers) and h-4 (Agriculture Labourers) groups. The few getting

131 Mor Singh a villager from Kondari shared that, in my life, first time I have seen Rs. 1,00,000 together. This amount I received as compensation for my two *bega* land. I do not know what to do with that, everyday what I get as wage I use to spend for our needs. I never keep money for tomorrow. It is not safe to keep more money. No one in my family have account in bank. We do not know how to read and write only our children know. I used to take alcohol. I started to drink more with friends after getting compensation. Still my wife is working as agriculture labourer in nearby villages and I also work in the field as well as in cities as contract labour. So we get grains from there for survival. With the compensation we may get only one or less than two *biga* land. That also we have to get in another village. It is difficult to look after the land that is away from my house. So I spend for drinking. Interview with Mor Singh, Agriculture labour, Kondari village, 7th May, 2008; some others mainly youngsters purchased bikes Interview with Aneez Ahmad, Village Chief, Kondari village, Kunderki Block, Moradabad, 7th May, 2008.

132 The study revealed the fact that the size of the land they have purchased with the compensation is less for 65% of the villagers, and the same size for 35%.

same amount of land are from the h-3 (Market-oriented Farmers) sections. Most of them agreed that the ground water come deeper from the land newly purchased than earlier.[133] When the holding of land resources become less, the income from the livestock is also less. Among them the most affected group is h-2 (Small Farmers) section. It is mainly because they kept more livestock before setting up zone and now they are not able to get fodder, which is mainly from land. Among those who have no change are mainly h-3 (Market-oriented Farmers), and h-4 (Agriculture Labourers) sections, because h-3 unit (Market-oriented Farmers) have access to land in nearby villages. So they could manage it. h-4 unit (Agriculture Labourers) was keeping fewer number of livestock. So, they are able to keep it now without any disruption.[134] This study shows that exercising control over resources have affected them badly, especially the Agriculture Labourers and Small/Subsistence Farmers (h-2 & h-4). As the h-2 unit loses their control over resources, they moved towards h-4 unit, mainly engaged in non-agriculture work and h-4 unit (Agriculture Labourers) also moved towards the same. Thus, the nature of work of both these units has changed.

The combined resources and labour explains the activity chain, mainly the relation of h-4 (Agriculture Labourers), h-3 (Market-oriented Farmers) and h-2 (Small Farmers) sections to the resources, i.e., land. The combination of resources and labour, in the area of agriculture, relates to the skill (to till land), wage, and employment days.

Before setting up the zone, these sections were mainly engaged in agriculture, in which land and water were the main resource. However, after setting up SEZ, most of them turn to resources like machines and similar things needing only unskilled labour power. They are mainly h-2 (Small Farmers) and h-4 (Agriculture Labourers) sections, who lost the access to the natural resources. The sections, whose condition of skill has not changed, are from h-3 (Market-

133 80% get water from deeper than previously. 20% do not have any change in their water availability situation.

134 Looking at income from the livestock, 55% have less than earlier. 45% do not have any change in the amount of their income.

oriented Farmers), who can still work in their newly purchased land, though size is less.[135]

Number of employment days also after setting up zone became less, it is because villagers are not able to get regular work instead they get contract work. Regarding the wage, though some get more money as wage than as agriculture labour, when it compares with expenses such as travel, food items, they get less income.

In addition to these, the nature of work also differs after setting up the zone. Earlier many were engaged mainly in family labour. They were highly skilled in agriculture work. Though, for some work time restrictions were there, mostly they were not restricted with time and they had leisure time. Now in cities, they are supposed to work in a limited space and have very little leisure time. They are strictly supervised by the owners. They are not skilled in this new work. They work now in a hazardous situation. Thus, the access to resources through labour get affected by deskilling, demeaning the dignity of labour by taking out their leisure time and by not keeping any basic amenities for labour. They only work via an agreement through a contractor, who extracts good percentage of their wage.

The claim of members on production has been changed. The researcher's study regarding the food habits and sources of food items shows that, before setting-up the zone, villagers were mainly dependent on the share of the production from their own field or the field where they work, where wage they received were mostly in terms of grains or pulses. So, the activity chain between these units connected to domestic or local circuit. Most of them got enough share for their survival. But, after setting up the zone, their claim on production is mainly limited to money, i.e., daily wage. So, the link between these units (h-1, h-2, h-3, and h-4) in the economy has changed. Now their main links have shifted to 'national' circuit; national circuit connects with international circuit. So, the price variations are always possible. It affected their work, which is mainly for necessitates. Thus, they moved towards a complex phenomenon. The study shows that, this complexity has affected them badly; they

135 85% have less wages and greater loss of skills after setting-up SEZ. 15% do not have any change. Regarding the employment days 75% have fewer days after setting-up SEZ and 25% do not have any change.

can't maintain their food habits with the limited income. The change in claims of members on production has adversely affected the Subsistence or Small Farmers (h-2 unit), and Agriculture labourers. It is mainly because for Small/Subsistence Farmers (h-2 unit) ownership of land was main resource while agriculture labourers lost their access to land as a labourer. The loss of resources affects their claims on production from the land. Nevertheless, market-oriented farmers (h-3 unit) are able to purchase some land elsewhere. So, that it helped them to keep their claims on production.

Only, the cultivable land has been acquired for SEZ. So, there was no direct displacement. There housing has not changed. There was also very less effect on education. Regarding health condition some of them are unaware regarding their health conditions. However, the researcher's observation as well as contact with the workers in the city gives an impression that the health condition of the employees in the unorganized sectors in Moradabad is acute & they are now subject to many diseases.

In brief, the trend of the field study shows that, all the sections of the samples have been adversely affected by loss of resources. However, the intensity of negative influence varies. The resources loss influence more on the Agriculture Labourers and Small Farmers, who were attached to land as employee and cultivator. It is because their minimal survival was attached to this livelihood base that can't be replaced. Though, they can interact with other units but those are not able to ensure their life and livelihood. At the same time though Market- oriented Farmers lost the resources they are able to keep some attachment to livelihood base. As they lose resources, their employees, i.e., Agriculture Labourers also lose the link to resources and employers.

3.2.3. Madurai Field Study

Madurai, known as the temple city, is situated into the central part of Tamil Nadu. Nowadays both central and state governments have planned to change the face of this city, so they have number of development programmes. At the same time, they have also planned to make this as a hub of export-oriented production, so the authorities acquire huge amount of land which is close to city and mainly belong to the villagers.

The researcher has conducted a study on one of these areas, Sivarikottai village, which the government has announced to be acquired for setting up Special Economic Zone.

The researcher has visited this place to know the status of the villagers' livelihood and the possible impact of the SEZ on it. For that he has taken a total of 20 samples, which are from various categories, namely, Market-oriented Farmers, Subsistence Farmers, and Agriculture Labourers. These categories were divided into different caste groups, who are dominant in each category, namely, Tevar (TR), Reddiyar (RR), Parayar (PR), Chakkliyar (CR), and Goundas (GS).

3.2.3.1. Present Status of the Land

The researcher has studied and collected information regarding the status of land. The research findings show, Appendix 3.15, that 2480 acres of land has been allocated for the SEZ in Sivarikottai; consisting of 76.22% of private land which is cultivable. 23.28% is common land. This is a government land; many of the villagers including landless engaged in cattle breeding, heavily depends on the common land, virtually this property belongs to the state government. 00.50% of land is covered by water bodies, which is the water source for cultivation.

3.2.3.2. Process and Procedures (Beginning stage) of SEZ

Though 2480 acres of land has been marked for setting up SEZ, no proper information has been given to the villagers and village officials. Present market value of this land depends on the closeness to the road, as per the data collected from the field, the land which is closer to road may cost Rs. 50,000 to Rs.100,000 per cent, the land which is a little distant from the road may cost Rs. 13,000 to Rs. 15,000 per cent, and the land which is far from the road may cost Rs. 1000 to Rs. 3000 per cent. Regarding the compensation, villagers have not received any information till now.

3.2.3.3. Condition of Existing Livelihood

The researcher has conducted a sample survey in order to find out the existing livelihood conditions. For that the subject has been divided into four: livelihood dependency, condition of the land, water availability, and the situation with wages, employment days, and skill.

3.2.3.3.1. Livelihood Dependency

The researcher has studied livelihood dependency to find out in which area: Agriculture, Non-agriculture or both villagers depend for their livelihood. The researcher's findings, in Appendix 3.8, show that concerning livelihood dependency, 95% (19 persons) depend more on agriculture. In a rural area normal people usually depends on Agriculture, it includes cultivation in all the seasons, especially here in two seasons, and if they get good rains, they can cultivate all the seasons, and many of them are involved in cattle breeding, and many landless Agriculture labourers depend on the common land for cattle breeding.

Only 5% (1 person) depend on both agriculture and construction work in the village and nearby places. And no one is dependent more on non-agriculture work, such as construction works and related works for their livelihood.

3.2.3.3.2. Condition of People's Land

The researcher's findings, in Appendix 3.9, on the condition of people's land are concerned with the nature of land, that are mainly of three kinds: Cultivatable in all seasons; throughout a year; Seasonal cultivatable: it can be cultivated only few seasons when monsoon water is available; and Non-Cultivatable: due to lack of water or of rocky nature this land can't be cultivated. The study shows that all agree that land is seasonally cultivatable. The water which is stored up during the seasons helps them to cultivate 9 ½ months in a year.[136]

136 Interview with Ramalingam Tewar, Subsistence farmer, Sivaraikottai village, 9th September, 2008.

3.2.3.3.3. Water Availability for Agriculture

The researcher's findings, in Appendix 3.10, show the water availability for agriculture. Everyone (100%) agreed that access to water is mainly dependant on rain (seasonal), i.e., from the ponds, there are five ponds; it covers 00.50% of total land. This is used for one yield and rest of the period for cotton, beans etc.[137]

3.2.3.3.4. Condition of Wage, Employment Days, and Skill

The researcher's findings, in Appendix 3.11, on the condition of wages, employment days, and skill is mainly based on the question that, in which area, Agriculture, Non-Agriculture or both, does one get more wages, more days of employment, and more skill? The study was conducted among two caste groups: Parayar, and Chakliyar who work mainly as agriculture labourers.

Regarding the employment days, 87.5% have more employment days in agriculture; they work in the field almost all the nine and half months and are also engaged in grazing the cattle of others.

12.5% have equal employment days in agriculture and non-agriculture. They work in construction site as well. And no one has more days work in non-agriculture.

Regarding the workers' skills, 87.5% have more skill in agriculture work than non-agriculture work, traditionally they were doing agriculture work, and did not need instruction in the agriculture field.

12.5% have skill in both agriculture and non agriculture work. And no one has more skill in non-agriculture work than agriculture work.

3.2.4. Analysis of field findings of proposed SEZ area at Sivarikottai in Madurai

The existing livelihood condition is depended mainly on Agriculture in this place. Here, for 9½ months land is used for agriculture. So, it is not so called 'waste land'. The common land is also used for grazing. So, the internal activities of the different units for their

137 Interview with Pandiayan, Market-oriented Farmer, Sivarikottai village, 14th May, 2008.

livelihood depend on land, both agriculture &, common, and water.[138] So change in ownership of resources will break the activity chain that ensures the livelihood of this village community. As the Agriculture Labourers (h-4 unit) they will not get any compensation; they are mainly Dalits, among them some depend on common land for grazing goat. Landholding communities will get compensation. Whether it is adequate enough to get same size of land or not is to be known later.

The combined resources and labour explains the activity chain, mainly the relation of h-4, h-3 and h-2 sections to the land. The combination of resources and labour, in the area of agriculture, relates to the skill (to till land), wage, and employment days.[139]

If their land is taken their economic activity chain will be affected. It will seperate these communities from their own land, and related culture, and community life because a major section may have to travel to cities to engage in other work, i.e., mainly construction work. The possible move they can make is to become an unskilled labour in the cities, where many threat waits for them.

Claims of members on the production are mostly now share of pulses and grains as wage, especially during the harvesting time. During the other time, they get wage. If the land is taken they may have to depend on everything in the market. Market will be fluctuating. It will affect the livelihood of these communities.

This field study shows that the most threatened units are Subsistence/small farmers (h-2 unit) and Agriculture Labourers (h-4 unit). As the former get a small compensation which will not mostly be enough to get the same amount of land and the latter will not get any compensation and existing employment will be lost. They can only move towards hazardous occupations with their labour power.

---

138 76.22% land is private and cultivatable for 9½ months. Water is available through pond which occupies 00.50% of the total land, i.e., 2480 acres. 95% depend more on agriculture in the village for livelihood.

139 Regarding the labour 87.5% get more working days, more wage (monthly income), and have more skill in agriculture. 12.5% do not have any change.

3.5. Major Findings of Field Study

The change of access to local resources has affected the livelihood of farming communities, specially Agriculture Laboures and Small Farmers. It is because:

- The land acquired for SEZ used for multiple crops as it has water resources.
- With the compensation, the Small farmers can't purchase same amount of land.

The people who had access to resources through labour were not being compensated.

- The Small Farmers and Agriculture Labourers moved towards non-agriculture work in industrial sector. It does not provide adequate provision for livelihood like earlier. On the contrary it endangers their very life, culture, skill, and so on.
- SEZ helps to expand the labour market by pushing away the farmers from their own livelihood base and forced them to seek for other means of livelihood. Thus, this policy helps to expand 'contractualisation' of labour and 'causalisation' of work and make available 'flexibility of labour'. Thus, SEZ that emphasis export growth destroys local economy and thereby livelihood of people.
- The development paradigm that gives open invitation to external and internal capital investment devalues the dignity of labour and nature of work. Thus it makes life and livelihood of rural folk more precarious.
- The state is no more a welfare state for the marginalized people. But a security state, who protect the cause of the rich.

Therefore, the protest of the marginalized against SEZ is a cry to recapture access over resources, regain dignity for work, and reclaim culture of life.

Conclusion

The major findings of the field study show that source of livelihood of these communities, has been acquired forcefully by giving less compensation. Consequently, they were forced to move towards cities, where they get work in sub-processing units of industry. This change forces them to become commodities in labour market, where they sell their labour power either as unskilled labour, contract labour, or as casual labour. As a result they are forced to be in a place where they are prone to get exploited. Neo-liberal economy systematically expands cheap labour market in the so called third world countries with the ardent support of the government. Thus, they succeeded in destroying domestic economy of people.

By looking at these problems on the one side and the slogan of more production on other side, various responses to SEZ can be seen, some response vigorously supporting and others vigorously opposing, and few seeking modification in the existing SEZ law. It will be discussed in detail in the next chapter.

Chapter IV

SEZ and Various Responses

Introduction

This chapter mainly deals with various responses to the livelihood question of Agriculture Labourers and Small Farmers. As we have discussed in chapter II, the livelihood question has been influenced by policy organizing agencies. The main policy organizing body is the government, which is formal legislative body and it represents major political parties. They represent different ideological strands. It can be generally divided as Rightists, Centralists and Leftists. The major question discussed in this chapter is how do the major political parties, and related trade unions, respond to the livelihood question of farming community? Besides this, the response of other influential agencies in the society such as Industrialists: Indian Chamber of Commerce and Federation of Indian Chamber of Commerce & Industry, and People's movements and its various ideological wings has also been examined.

4.1. Peoples' Livelihood and Economic Paradigm of Major Political Parties

The question of livelihood is always related to the paradigm of development. Nowadays, all the major political parties in India stress 'Neo-liberal development model.' But they emphases differently. The rightist supports the Indian Corporate to come out. It can be called 'Liberalization of economy mostly with Indian Corporate.' The Centrist emphasizes the slogan 'liberalization with human face', but usually it is a political tool to appeal the mass. The Left is now in between their ideology and 'corporate capitalism.'

This model emphases the industrialization and believes that it would solve the livelihood issues. But how do they react when the livelihood problem of agrarian communities is intensified under this economic paradigm of development? It is a challenging question which is usually used as a political tool to attack the ruling party.

On one side, the leading political parties treat natural resources as a means for the profit maximization, and on the other side all the political parties address the livelihood question of farmers. Thus, all the major national parties and regional parties from different ideological strands strive for two irreconcilable goals. Some of the major statements of the political parties regarding the livelihood question are:

4.2. Rightist Political Party

4.2.1. Bharatiya Janata Party

The Bharatiya Janata Party (BJP) (Indian People's Party), founded in 1980, is one of the major political party in India. The party advocates conservative social policies, robust economic growth, foreign policy driven by a nationalist agenda, and strong national defense. The party has a strong relation with the *Sangh Parivar* in which the *Rashtriya Swayamsevak Sangh* plays a leading role. BJP came powerfully into the national politics in late eighties. In 1996, they came to power for a short period. Then in 1998 they formed a coalition government. During this time BJP government introduced SEZ. It was the then Commerce Minister Murosali Marar who proposed this policy after his visit to China.

The BJP's position on SEZ is not different with the Congress party. The muddled ideological basis for the BJP prescription to the SEZ issue is another reminder on how the principal opposition fails the Right of Center test when it comes to economic issues. All state governments in which they rule implemented SEZ policy without much difference from the central government.

They seek review on certain matters of this policy. They had concern for land. It says, SEZs should have a minimum area, limited acquisition of farm land, no development of residential real estate, and high compensation rates and locations that are not proximate to metros.[140]

In an interview, former finance minister and BJP leader Yasvant Sinha criticized that,

> "SEZs are almost foreign territories, so, we should have had one SEZ in every state, maybe two in a larger state. But you cannot have hundreds of SEZs in the country...(if so) it is nothing but a real estate scam. The current model will displace people. We have to take jobs to the people rather than take away the jobs and make people migrate".[141]

Regarding Land Acquisition Act he said that, "The Land Acquisition Act[142] should be used only for government projects, and, if necessary, public sector projects such as road or railway line, for that we need land. So, "go to the people and pay for it. But acquiring land for the private sector is not a good idea." Thus BJP, though supportive to SEZ, some of the questions related to land, they oppose. But, the state in which they rule failed to practice what they profess.

---

140 "BJP is likely to support SEZ policy", *Times News Network* (26 Jan, 2007), Http//: times ofindia.indiatimes. com /article show/402189.cms - 65k (5 Nov 2008).

141 Interview with Yaswanth sinha by Shantanu Guha Ray, cited in, "Take Jobs to People Don't Take Their Jobs And Force Migration", Bharath Versus India --Featured Paper, www.tehelka.com/story main31.asp? filename=Bu160607 Punditspeak_(Jun 16, 2007).

142 Present government goes against this idea and drafts a business-friendly Land Acquisition Act.

4.3. Centralist Political Parties

4.3.1. Indian National Congress

Indian National Congress, the ruling party headed by Ms. Sonia Gandhi, moves forward with the so called neo-liberal policies. The present government headed by Manmohan Singh introduced SEZ Act.

However, due to the rise of various concerns and agitation of farmers, Sonia Gandhi, the President of Congress party said that "good farm land should not be diverted for industry and wherever possible SEZ should come up on wasteland or not very good farm land",[143] and also announced a suspension of all land acquisition for establishing new SEZs until a new policy on the rehabilitation of displaced people is announced.[144]

But party can't make any step for the betterment of farmers, though various concerns were raised from few corners. At the same time, it was concerned about the promoters whose projects were notified and recommended for de-notification before the Union Commerce Ministry by the State Government in Goa.[145] It is very evident that all the state governments which are ruled by Congress party promote SEZ, except Goa, where it was due to people's strong resistance from the peoples groups. The Party sells the land of farmers to the corporate, and sees the land as commodity rather than the means of livelihood.

4.3.2. Regional and Other National Political Parties

Among the major regional parties who took initiative to promote SEZ at the cost of farmers are: *Dravida Munnetta Kazhakam* (DMK) which fully supports SEZ policy. It acquires forcefully and sells

143 Quoted in "Zones of Conflict", *Down To Earth*, (Nov. 15, 2006): 23.

144 Praful Bidwai, "India: Special Economic Zones on the Backburner", *IPS* (Feb 12, 2007), 1 of 3, http://www. ipsnews.net/news.asp? idnews =36523 (5 Nov 2008).

145 "Congress party favours compensating SEZ promoters in Goa", *Economic Times* (19 Jul, 2008), http://www.Economictimes.indiatimes.com/News/PoliticsNation/ Congress_party_favours_compensating_ SEZ...in_Goa /.../3252937.cms (5th Nov., 2008).

people's livelihood base to the corporate.[146] *Telengu Dessam Party* (TDP) and *Biju Janata Dal* (BJD) supports SEZ policy.

Some of the regional parties who opposed land acquisition of SEZ policy are: *Rashtriya Janata Dal* (RJD) criticizes this policy. Party leader and Union Rural Development Minister Prasad Singh terms the promotion of SEZ as a 'land scam'. According to him, the SEZs serve as a ploy to hand over huge tracts of agriculture land to corporate bigwigs.[147] *Pattali Makkal Kashi* (PMK) criticizes the central and Tamil Nadu government, Union Minister R. Ramadoss organized seminar along with *Pasumaithaygam Ammayippu* (Green House Organization), which discuss the various problem related to SEZ.[148] *Trinamul Congress* and *Janta Dal* (Secular) oppose this policy. AIADMK chief Jayalalitha said that she will lead an agitation against the SEZ project in Tamil Nadu "as it is a bid to destroy the livelihood of farmers" [149] Late *Jan Morcha* leader and former Prime Minister Viswanath Pratap Singh called for a six month moratorium on the implementation of the Act during which time new regulatory mechanism would be in place for SEZs.[150]

Most all these parties oppose atrocities against farmers, especially if they are in opposition.

4.4. Leftist Parties

There are two left factions discussed here: CPI (M), CPI

4.4.1. Communist Party of India (Marxist)

The communist parties generally support the working class and farmers. It opposes the intervention of external forces and corporates.

146 Solai, "Pulikalku Swathanthram Tharum Poluthurale Mandalangal", ed. by. A. Joseph Raj, *Sirappu Porulathara Mandalam Ezhkalil Meethe Thakkam* (Special Economic Zone Affects the Poor) (Uthukadu: Kasa People Centre for Alternative, 2006), 18.

147 Venkitesh Ramakrishanan, "Conflict Zones", *Frontline*, 7.

148 J. Vadivelu, "Vevasaya Nilangalkku Vettu", ed. by. A. Joseph Raj, *Sirappu Porulathara Mandalam Ezhkalil Meethe Thakkam,* 13-14.

149 "Tata's Tamil Nadu project runs into opposition from villagers" *Indian Express* (Chennai), 30 July 2007, 4.

150 Venkitesh Ramakrishanan, "Conflict Zones", *Frontline*, 8.

It theoretically opposes the commoditization of resources. So, party brought out strong statements against this trend. The statement of Politbureau issued on 18th January, 2007 says[151] that, "a complete and comprehensive rehabilitation policy has to be announced for those people whose land would be acquired for SEZ area."

In Himachal Pradesh, Tamil Nadu, Maharashtra CPI (M) launched a mass campaign against the dangers of SEZs. Specially, their demand emphasized the resource base protection of the farmers.[152] Those are:

- The government sells prime agriculture land for SEZ.
- Selling the land at throw away prices.
- Land is becoming non-remunerative and peasantry is becoming landless.
- Displacement of farmers.
- Giving very meager amount as compensation.
- Adequate steps to compensate and rehabilitate the displaced people must be taken.

So, CPI (M) demanding urgent changes in the SEZ Acts and Rules. In his speech at Vidharbha region in Maharashtra, CPI (M) Secretary Prakash Karat said "the peasantry is being fleeced by the

---

151 It also addresses some matters those are: Firstly, the highest limit of land to be used for a definite industry has to be fixed. An article is to be included in the SEZ Act regarding the use of land –so that 50% of land is used for the production and processing of the commodities of the factory and 25% of the land is used for infrastructural development-this has to be made compulsory. Secondly, the proposed concessions (including different tax acts and others) for SEZ will have to be withdrawn. Thirdly, the application of labour laws within the SEZ area must be made mandatory; Party to Launch mass Against SEZs," *Peoples Democracy* 1/28 (October 9-15, 2006): 5-6; Kushal, Debnath, "SEZ Act and CPI (M)," *Janata* 62/16 (May, 2007): 12-15.

152 Other demands are: 25% of the land in multi product SEZs are to be set aside for industry/processing. This means 75% of the land is for the promoter to make huge profits.

The stipulation of the land to be used in a SEZ for industry must be increased to at last 50% and 25% for related infrastructure.

Tax exemptions must be drastically pruned. "Party to Launch mass Against SEZs," *Peoples Democracy* 1/28 (October, 09-15, 2006): 6.

SEZ policy which has to be resisted".[153] At Konkan Bhavan in Navi Mumbai, in a rally, Sitaram Yechury, the Polit Bureau member, attacked the central government for initiating and going ahead with SEZ plans in various states with no concern whatsoever for the interest of the peasantry.[154]

However, the states in which they rule, implemented SEZ policy without much change. And also in West Bengal they used state force and party cadres to repress the farmer's opposition, even to the extent of killing them.

4.4.2. Communist Party of India

CPI opposes the existing SEZ law, because it ignores the labour law, so how it can be beneficial to the larger portion of population, who are workers. Majority of the established SEZs in the country require highly technically man power. Local population works as contract labour earning per day Rs. 50-100. They are mostly semi-skilled or illiterate and do not have any right to form a union or bargain for their wages, not even talking about benefits like health, work and place accident insurance. So, the claim of central government that SEZ would create more employment is a myth.[155]

They also say SEZ Act does not contain single clause to protest the rights of the farmers from who the required land has been acquired, and no rehabilitation measures have been suggested for the displaced sections of rural population.[156]

So, CPI demands today's industrialization should not be carried out on the expense of livelihoods of local population in the name of high economic growth and profits. Similarly, land acquisition policy should be democratic by reaching a consensus dialogue with farmers' local *Gram Sabhas* rather than forceful land grabbing. Also establishment of high-tech industries with low employment rate

---

153 Ashoka Dhawale, "Massive Peasant Rallies Attack Government Policies Leading To Peasant Suicide and SEZs," *Peoples Democracy* 1/28 (October 9-15, 2006): 8.

154 Ibid., .8-9.

155 Soma Sunder. M, "SEZ and Turmoil in Rural India," *New Age* 56/35 (August 31-September 6, 2008): 5, 12.

156 Ibid.

should be shunned. The state should realize that the country belongs not only to a handful of industrial houses but also to millions of people and the right to life of these sections should be ensured.[157]

Thus, CPI differs with its trusted ally CPI (M) in West Bengal and Kerala.

4.5. Trade Unions Trade Unions

4.5.1. Central India Trade Union

CITU is affiliated with Communist party of India (Marxist). General Secretary of CITU, Dipankar Mukherjee in his letter to the committee on subordinate Legislation in *Rajya Sabha* sought for immediate intervention in respect of various Provisions in the SEZ Act.[158] Some of the provisions which address the resources base follow:

- Our constitution doesn't permit formation of a state within the state. But the SEZ Act permits ownership of land without any ceiling to developers.
- SEZ Act prescribe the minimum area of land (section 3 (8)), but doesn't say about the maximum limit.
- There is no specific mention in the Act about the ownership of the land, taken over by the state for the purpose of setting up of SEZ. So, the rule should specify that land given to the developers will be of lease hold nature only.
- In the SEZ Act section 5 (1) (a) says that notification of any SEZ shall be guided by the generation of

157 Ibid. In addition, they sought intervention for Minimum land use for processing area now is 25% of the total SEZ area; it may lead to real estate business. So, CITU demand total processing area should be kept 50% of total area.

SEZ Act, specified the function of Development Commission, but the rules provide enormous power to him/her disproportionate to functions assigned to him under the Act. Such unbridled power without accountability would be utilized by the developers/management crush all democratic movements including the right to form association and union and the right to move freely as mandated under Article 19 of the constitution. And cost benefit analysis is necessary. Ibid.

158 "SEZ Rules Violate Constitution: CITU Petitions Committee on Subordinate Legislation," *Peoples Democracy* 1/28 (October 09-15, 2006): 7, 9.

additional economic activity and creation of employment opportunity. The same cannot be achieved if there is a serious social unrest, likely to erupt without specific guidelines on land compensation/rehabilitation package. Therefore, in order to avoid social unrest there must be specific rules with regard to; the modalities of land, and granting compensation for the land losers and Agriculture Labourers.

- The clauses 5 (e), (f) and (g) under section 5 should be fully deleted from the rules. As it allows the delegation of power to Development Commissioner on labour related issues. It should only be related with existing labour laws of the land.

CITU, one of the leftist-favored trade union demands above changes in the SEZ Act. It is mainly to protect the livelihood of farming community and labourers.

4.5.2. All India Trade Union Congress

AITUC, affiliated with Communist Party of India, supported struggle of Farmers in Pune District.[159] In Orissa, AITUC demands a protest against the proposed project in Kalinga Nagat. AITUC General Secretary Gurudas Dasgupta said that "our members will mobilize support for a discussion in Parliament to ensure that the anti-national deal gets exposed, and in no circumstances would his organization allow agricultural land to be utilized for industrial purposes."[160]

4.5.3. Indian National Trade Union Congress

INTUC, trade union wing of Congress party, generally agree with the policies of Congress government though they have doubt about labour related issues as a Trade Union. However, in Kerala, they have urged the Communist government to set up a statutory tripartite body to handle labour issues in SEZ. The body comprised of government

159 Sampat Kale, "Defeat SEZ Policy," *Janata* 61/36 (October 15, 2006): 9.

160 "AITUC demands white paper on POSCO" *The Hindu* (Bhuvaneswar), 28 May, 2007, 4.

officials, representatives of trade unions and managements should be given power to ensure job security, workers right and privileges.[161] Unlike other trade unions INTUC doesn't worry much about farmer's issues.

4.5.4. Bharatiya Mazdoor Sangha

BMS, the trade union wing of Bharatiya Janata Party, has warned that the SEZs will not only cause large amount of loss to the government but also affect the sovereignty of the nation.

> K Vishwanatha Shetty, BMS leader in Karnataka, says that "as the land given for the foreign companies under SEZ is free of control from various indigenous legislations, the government will lose control over the companies, and consequently the integrity and sovereignty of the nation will be in crisis. SEZs will become 'special exploitation zones'. SEZs are forcing the country to lose a large area of fertile land, thus to create an imbalance in the population growth and food supply in the forthcoming years." [162]

BMS's concerned about the lakhs of people belonging to the families of agriculturalists, artisans who will be unemployed with the establishment of more number of tech-based industries. Cottage and small scale industries will be ruined to within a few years, the protesters stated. [163]

4.6. Indian Federation of Chamber of Commerce and Industry (FICCI), Confederation of Indian Industry (CII)

The manner in which a large number of SEZ proposals have come up in areas adjoining urban centers, CII noted that this is a cause of

161 "Set up Body to Handle Labour Issues in SEZs says INTUC", *The Hindu* (Madurai), 14 October, 2008, 7.

162 SEZs will affect sovereignty of nation", *Deccan Herald* (26 July, 2007), www.deccanherald.com /CONTENT/Jul262007/district2007072515174.asp - 68k (5 November, 2008).

163 Ibid.

worry. CII president R. Sesha Sayee says the focus of SEZs should be on labour intensive manufacturing[164]. Bibek Debroy, the Secretary General of Indian Chamber of Commerce and Industry, says "it s look probable that SEZs will be used for freeing land for real estate through a back door".[165] He adds that this approach may increase regional differences.

All the major political parties and trade unions address on one side the livelihood issues of farming communities while on the other side they support the expansion of industrialization. It is the deliberate attempt to cover the issue of farmer's livelihood question, which is essentially connected with the development paradigm. In this context, people's movements launch massive struggle against the neo-liberal economic paradigm, that is the primary cause for the destruction of livelihood base of agrarian communities.

4.7. People's Movements

People's movement in their approaches and views differ from each other. Following ways it is divided: Neo Gandhians, Neo-Marxists, and Neo-Ambedkarites. But one major body of organizations (NAPM), includes all these ideological categories.

4.7.1. Neo-Marxists

The followers of this ideological category follow Marxian principles. They oppose the commoditization of resources and labour power. They resist capitalism with violent revolutionary approaches. The major movements in this group are Communist Ghadar Party of India, and Communist Party (Marxist-Leninist).

4.7.1.1. Communist Ghadar Party of India

The Party's official Magazine, Peoples' Voice, points out the dangerous factors of SEZ, and opposes leading communist parties;

Firstly, those who compromise with the drive of the big capitalists to grab agricultural land says that 'this is alright' provided that the peasants are willing to sell their land and the state gives them

---

164 S. Viswanathan and Venkitesh Ramakrishanan, "At a Crossroads," *Frontline* 23/24 (December 2-15, 2006): 8.

165 Quoted in "Not Wasted," *Down to Earth* (November 15, 2006): 26.

'fair compensation'[166]. Leaving aside the question of whether or not the peasants really gave up their land *willingly*, this position fails to defend the general social interest. It ignores the fact that conversion of agricultural land for non-agricultural use, driven by the greed of big capitalists, endangers food security. It also endangers human life itself, by reducing the green cover that produces the oxygen required by human beings.

Secondly, there are those who demand that the state must not intervene in the land transaction, but leave it to the 'free market'. This position, while pretending to be 'pro-farmer', actually plays into the hands of the big capitalists. The big corporations will get the land they want, and even if the peasants get a better price for their land, they would have lost their source of livelihood. Moreover, purchase of more and more cultivable land by the big capitalists for non-agricultural use will reduce the area under cultivation. Thus, this second trend is only a variation of the first. While the followers of this trend oppose the colonial Land Acquisition Act, they compromise on the question of permitting big capitalist profiteers to acquire whatever land they set their eyes on.

Thirdly, there is an argument that land under multiple cropping must be protected but land under a single crop can be acquired for SEZs. Of the total area cultivated in the country, only one-third is sown more than once, while two-thirds have only a single crop. To protect only one-third of the cultivated land means in effect no protection at all. It means to allow most of the cultivable land to be freely converted for other use.

Fourthly, there is an argument that SEZs are alright provided the land that is acquired by the state is not sold but leased out to the big capitalists. This is the latest argument of the CPI (M) in the debate that is raging over the question of land acquisition for industry and for SEZs.[167] This position compromises with SEZs, as it does not even raise the question as to what is special about them,

166 This is one of the main arguments advanced by the Left Front Government in West Bengal, for instance, to justify the acquisition of peasants' land by the Tatas at Singur.

167 Example Kerala Smart city SEZ, here land is leased out to Dubai based company.

and why do they deserve special privileges. It also compromises with the colonial Land Acquisition Act, accepting the unlimited right of the state to acquire any land it pleases for any purpose whatsoever, disregarding the right of the tiller of the land to a secure livelihood. It also ignores the fact that big capitalists get away with selling even 'lease-hold' land in the existing system, as they did with the mill lands in Mumbai.

So, in order to defend the rights of workers and peasants, and the general interests of the society, it is necessary to oppose the SEZ Act without any compromise. It is necessary to demand not only that the SEZ Act as well as the Land Acquisition Act be immediately scrapped, but also that a new law be passed that would ban any private company from purchasing any piece of land.

CGP Leaders ask, what will be the result, if land use is left to be determined by the so-called market forces? More and more land will be transferred into the hands of the biggest capitalist monopolies. This is a dangerous trend. It endangers the availability of housing and shelter, food security, as well as protection of the natural environment. Purchase of land by private capitalist corporations must therefore be immediately halted.

People of each state, and of each city, must take control of how land is used within the territory they live in, through elected representatives who they control. Land must be allocated according to a social plan, taking into account the different needs. It must be leased out to different users, whose right to possess the land would be conditional on their fulfilling their committed obligation to use the land in harmony with the general interests of the society.

Land that is cultivable must be protected. This includes the area that is currently cultivated and the area that is possible to bring under cultivation through appropriate investments. This requires legislation and enforcing mechanisms to ban the conversion of cultivable land for non-agricultural use. Land for industrial, housing and other non-agricultural use can and must be identified from within the 1,93,000 hectares of 'barren and uncultivable land' that is available in the country, according to official data.

It is in the interests of workers, peasants, women and youth, the peoples of all nationalities, tribes and forest communities, to take an uncompromising position against the SEZ Act and demand that both SEZ Act and the Land Acquisition Act are not acceptable in its implementation – in defense of the rights of all workers and peasants, and in the general interests of society.[168]

4.7.1.2. Communist Party of India (ML)

CPI (ML) is people's movement began to address peacefully on people's issues such as land, livelihood and liberation from feudal and imperial exploitation and oppression. But, now they use violent method for their cause; they say that, it is mainly because we were not heeded and were violently repressed by the state.[169]

In his speech at the 8th Congress at Kolkata Dipankar Bhattacharya, General Secretary of CPI (ML) said that "The SEZ Act was passed in Parliament unanimously, with not a single vote against the SEZ Act from the partners of either NDA or UPA, or even the entire brigade of more than 60 Left MPs. The West Bengal Government imagined that this Act can be a foundation for the state's industrialization policy. But in a development that no one expected, the peasants of Nandigram challenged the power of the entire Parliament, and the State Government which enjoys a massive majority in the State Assembly. This was the power of the people that all the power of the state failed to defeat. Without this power of the people there can be no Left politics. It is this power of the people that we are gathered here to uphold, defend and consolidate."[170]

Singur and Nandigram and struggles against SEZs have in fact rekindled a Left urge wide-ranging. In 1967, India had felt the need

168 "Uncompromisingly oppose the anti-social SEZ Act! Rights of workers and peasants are inviolable!", People's Voice (English Fortnightly) (1-15 February, 2007), http//www.cgpi.org (5 November, 2008); "Peasant Struggle against Forcible Land Acquisition", *People's Voice* 30/19 (October 1-15, 2008): 8; "No to Forcible Acquisition of Agricultural Land, No to the Land Acquisition (amendment Bill) Bill," *Peoples Voice* 30/3 (February 1-15, 2008): 11.

169 Satarupa Bhattacharjya,"Red Terror," *India Today* 33/6 (February 5-11, 2008): 33.

170 "A Congress of Great Resolve for a Big Push Forward", http//:www.cpiml.org /liberation /year 2008/january/8thparty congress.html. (January, 2009)

for revolution. In 2007, again India seems to be looking with hope and eagerness for a revolutionary Left alternative.[171]

In the final section of the Kolkata meeting a resolution was passed which called for bold championship of the new signs and spirit of class and mass unity that were being seen across the country against the onslaught of imperialist globalization, especially against the SEZ policy and deprivation of the poor from their rightful claim to NREGA and BPL benefits, and a vigorous resistance to the assaults on secularism, democracy, national independence and sovereignty.[172]

Former General Secretary of CPI (ML) Muppala Laxmana Roa says "UPA government's SEZ policy aimed at creating 'Neo-colonial' enclaves'. So party members have mobilized people against proposed SEZs in Nandigram, Singur, Kalinga Nagar and other places...the word SEZ became a dirty word among the villagers of Dhurli and Bhansi (in Orissa)"[173]

Thus, both Neo-Marxist movements in India vigorously oppose SEZ and emphasize domestic or local economy. As they treat resources as base of livelihood as well as its bio-diversity, they oppose any step of government to see resources are commodities.

4.7.2. Neo-Ambedkarites

Neo-Ambedkarites approach to land evolved from Ambedkar's involvement with the struggle for the Dalits. Ambedkar encouraged small holdings, instead of keeping large farms by *Zamindars* and corporate farming.[174] He also fought for the rights of Dalit Agriculture Labourers. He opposed all the exploitative practice of land holding communities.[175] Thus, he treated land as a means of livelihood. Many Neo-Amberkrites fight against SEZ, though mainly they work along with other movements.

171 "A Congress of Great Resolve for a Big Push Forward", http//:www.cpiml.org /liberation /year 2008/january/8thparty congress.html. (January, 2009)

172 Ibid.

173 Satarupa Bhattacharjya, "Red Terror", 33-34.

174 Gail Omvedt, *Dalits and Democratic Revolution* (New Delhi: Sage Pub., 1994), 156-157.

175 Gail Omvedt, *Ambedkar: Towards an Enlightened India* (New Delhi: Penguin Books, 2004), 78.

In Karnataka, *Bhoomi Thayi Raitara Samithi* (The Farmer's Association of Mother Earth), an organization of farmers and *Dalit Sangharsh Samithi* (DSS), organized meetings among the farmers to create awareness about government policies on industrial and urban development that are inimical to the interests of farmers. Apart from opposing land acquisition by KIDAB for industrial purposes, the *samithi* is fighting against land acquisition by Mysore Urban Development Authority (MUDA).[176] Along with many people's movements Dalit movements are also part of this.

4.7.3. National Alliance for Peoples Movements

National Alliance for People Movement is the body that organizes different movements in India together which generally opposes all the people related questions and accommodates all the grass-root groups as well as some mass movements. Many issue based organizations are part of NAPM, which supports as well as helps them to organize themselves. NAPM organized Action 2007 and *Sangarsh* 2007 in order to resist different issues including Special Economic Zone.[177]

They oppose generally the Neo-liberal policies of the government; The policy framework that allows private control over community resources- water, biodiversity, forests seeds, agriculture markets, and mineral resources. So, they oppose Special Economic Zones. Some main arguments related to resource base follow: [178]

---

176 "Farmers up against land acquisition" *The Hindu* (Banglore), 6 July, 2007, 4

177 Medha Patker and Others, "UPA's Betrayal," *Janata* 62/12 (April 15, 2007): 15-16; Simpreet Singh, "Sangarsh 2007," *Janata* 62/12 (April 15, 2007): 16.

178 Medha Patkar and Amit Bhaduri, "Industrialisation," *The Movement of India* 2/2 (March-April, 2007): 6-8. Some general arguments are: The bias against the poor in policy making is both direct and indirect: the direct bias is visible in plan allocation. The direct bias operates pervasively through a pattern of consumption and production promoted by the state. In the metropolitan cities around 25% to 60% live in slums. Here, we need first basic amenities for the most needy, but governments are much worried for the improving quality of life of the rich and middle class. And promotes modes of transportation and all the facilities in order to attract the big corporate, they wants to produce for the rich and middle class. So, the poor do not get good facilities and now government want to promote this culture they want to take towards the villages, where the poor lives freely.

- Land is the primary source of livelihood in the agrarian economy. And large amount of Indian population depend on it.
- Land is the resource base (water, minerals etc.,) of rural community.
- This policy will attribute greater values to the selected products, which only the rich can buy, and the corporations can produce through large-scale destruction of livelihoods in both urban and rural areas.
- There will be large amount of agriculture refugees in the cities.[179] They will be further disadvantaged by the beautification policies of the government.
- It will be a threat to food security and environment.
- It will lead to social unrest.
- In the name of wealth creation and economic development the forces of economic degradation forces plunder our natural resources and cheat the local communities.[180]

The experience of earlier Export Processing Zone is to be taken into account, the track record is dismal. See Appendix 3. 13, 14, export growth and underemployment growth in EPZ.

In these Zones, as per the report of International Confederation of Free Trade Unions (ICFTU) in relation to the SEZ in other countries, "employers who run free-like a fox in a henhouse". Quoted in Muktar Srivastava, "Foxes have been Let Loose in the Hen House," *The Movement of India* 1/4 (July-August, 2006): 2.

While the farmers/unorganized sector workers are not given due prices for the produce, decent wages, social security benefits and subsidy, quoting the rules of WTO or availability of funds, the corporate are being given such wide range of concessions. Devender Sharma, "Displacing Farmers," *The Movement of India* 2/2 (March-April, 2007): 12.

Most of the SEZs in India are related with Information Technology sector, wealth creation in IT sector is not merely accumulation of labour, it is also based on exploiting international draconian legal framework of patents and intellectual property rights-whereby revenue is generated multiple time from a single labour. Ashim Roy and Others, "Smart City, Kerala," *Janata* 62/12 (April 15, 2007): 7.

People's movements under the leaders of NAPM demand sustainable and decentralized industrialization. Ibid.

179 Devender Sharma, "Displacing Farmers," 12.

180 Ibid., 3.

- The land ceiling reforms which were to benefit the Dalits, the landless have not been implemented anywhere, but instead there is full support to the land acquisition by private companies and developers.[181]
- SEZ is not simply industrialization it is a war against the simple living, generation old communities who are feeding the country. So, NAPM seeks "Special Justice Zones".[182]

Under the leadership of NAPM team many protests have been organized.

Leading Struggle of Movements/Peoples groups against SEZ in India: The farmers in the Raigad District of Maharashtra are involved with a long battle against a gigantic and powerful company Reliance, which earmarked 10,120 hectre of land for SEZ, out of that 5720 ha. are irrigated from Hetavane dam, and large tracts belong to the salt pans or wetlands, mangroves are very essentials for carrying capacity and sustainability of this area. In June, 2006, SEZ *Virodhi Sangarsh Samiti* (group which struggle against SEZ), and Peasant and Workers Party with its leader N. D Patil led a protest against the forcible acquisition of land by the state government for the Reliance company. There was police firing on that rally[183]. In this place, women farmers also led indefinite fast against Reliance Maha Mumbai SEZ.[184]

The farmers of eight villages in Delhi; Karala, Sultanpur Dabad, Tikri Khurd, Tikri Kalan, Alipur Bakauli and Kanjhawla were to lose their land for the purpose of industrial and residential complexes without consulting or informing the land owners and seeking their consent. This led to the dissatisfaction within the farmers who finally came out openly in protest when the amount

---

181 Devender Sharma, "Displacing Farmers," 3.

182 Ibid.

183 Sanjay Sangvai, "This Time Land-Grab by Rich," *The Movement of India* 1/2 (July-August, 2006): 4; "SEZ: Raigad Farmers Continue Protest," *The Hindu* (Madurai), 18 June, 2008: 4.

184 Surekha Dalvi, "Women Farmers Lead Indefinite Fast Against Reliance Mahamumbai SEZ," Janata 62/27 (July 29, 2007): 6.

of compensation was announced. Most of the villagers depend on Agriculture for their livelihood[185]. Though Delhi government has increased the compensation, but it is less than market value. So, the farmers have intensified their struggle and have now demanded complete de-notification of the land acquisition.[186]

In Tamil Nadu, at Tiruvanamallai, government wished to expand Cheyyar Special Economic Zone; for that they planned to acquire 2200 acres of land. The villagers started to protest and holding agitation under the banner of the *Sirappu Porulaathara Mandala Ethirpu Eyakam* (The Union Against SEZ). Most of the marked land is under cultivation now. They passed a resolution at the Gandhi Jayanti day against the government move to acquire land. It says, though Gandhi wanted to promote village economy that is mainly based on agriculture, today agriculture land is being taken away for SEZs throughout India[187]. The fact finding team of this union found out that the land acquired for SEZ includes the Bhoodan land, which was given to the landless as part of Land Reform.[188]

In Orissa at Kalinganagar (Jajpur district) Commerce Minister has given SEZ status to several Mineral-based (mainly Bauxite and other minerals) industries and information technology parks in the state. Here, local tribal people are facing eviction from their land. The *Visthapan Virodhi Janmanch*, local people's organization is spearheading the agitation,[189] especially against the POSCO project, which covers 6,000 acres, mostly agriculture land.

185 "Agitating farmers from Kanjhawala demands denotification of their lands"-- Featured Paper, http://mail.sify.com/readmail.php3?sessid=sicea3ac.(14 October, 2008)

186 Ibid.

187 Madhumita Dutta, "Will Cheyyar be TN's Nandigram?" (6 October, 2008), circular letter to csatts@sify.com (6 October, 2008).

188 Report of Public Enquiry of *Sirappu Porulaathara Mandala Ethirpu Eyakam* (Special Economic Zone opposing Association) (Chennai: Sirappu Porulaathara Mandala Ethirpu Eyakam, 2008) 2ff.

189 Prafulla Das, "Rural Resistance: Tribal Ire," *Frontline* 23/20 (October 7-20, 2006): 10-12.

Victory of People's Movement against SEZ: Singur in West Bengal was the one of the notable success of the struggle of people's movement against corporate giant Tata and state government. This area was thickly populated by mostly farming rural communities; agriculturists (land holding farmers and agriculture labourers), artisans, small traders, and other self employed people like share croppers, land migrants and resident labourers. When West Bengal government allotted 1000 acres of land for this project, local started to resist by organizing different forms of struggle. They were supported by human rights' groups, social activists & their organization's and political parties like Trinamool Congress and Socialist Unity Centre of India (SUCI), who played major role mobilizing people. Singur based mass organization, *Krishi Bhumi Raksha* (Agriculture Land Protectors) and the *Pachim Banga Khet Mazdoor Samiti* (West Bengal Agriculture Labourer Organization) and other people's movements protested strongly and eventually they were brutally repressed by state government and many protesters were killed by the police firing. Meanwhile many like-minded movements came together and continued to protest[190]. Due to the continue struggle, Tata Motors withdrew their Nano car project from the land of Singur that belongs to the people. The conflict that was avoided with this decision after many ups and downs and threats and promises was not just between the opposition party and the CPI (M) led Government of West Bengal as they tried to depict, but was rather one between the state and its people. The prime, irrigated and agricultural land of Singur was restored back to the hardworking rural communities.[191]

NAPM statement also asks Tata to follow democratic process and seek the consent of communities and not just the state before its cars or machines enter the land and before it makes any agreement with the state. And what is questioned here is the imposition of an undue push given to the corporate culture as against people's interest.

---

190 Mahasweta Devi and Others, "The Public Hearing and Further Investigation on the Struggle by the People of Singur," *Janata* 61/46 (December 24, 2006): 8-9; Pachim Banga Khet Majoor Samiti, "Singur:Facts and Untruths," *Frontier* 39/25 (January 7-13, 2007): 7.

191 Mukta Srivastava, "Statement on Singur", (3 October, 2008). Circular letter to scats@sify.com (3 October, 2008).

The displaced and deprived have and will have, the right to assert their decision if the state does not follow the democratic process. Statement concludes with a strong assertion and call that is "Singur also once again proves that everything that industries do, whether in the form of SEZ of forcible acquisition of land is not legitimate and this must hence forth be remembered by all the parties".[192]

In Tamil Nadu, at Solangurni in Madurai, SEZ was de-notified due to the continuous struggle of *Pennurimai Iyakkam* (Women's Union), a movement for women's rights, mainly under the leadership of Gabriela Dietrich, who is one of the founder of Madurai *Pennurmai Iyakkam*, and National convener of NAPM. They organized struggle along with Construction workers Union and later joined with *Deshiya Murpok Drawida Kazakam* Party. However, it says that it was de-notified because there was lack of ground water.[193]

Goa became the first state to successfully fight against SEZs and force the government to reject all the 15 SEZs in the state. The struggle was led by *SEZ Virodhi Manch*, (it is a people's movement against SEZ, supported by various NGOs like the council for social justice and peace, *Jagrut Goem*, and *Goa Bachao Abhiyan*). SVM obtained information through Right To Information Act and found out that no assessment studies has conducted about the possible challenges on the village people due to the setting up of the SEZ by the state government. So, they opposed SEZ on the following grounds:-[194]

- The allocation of land was done in a hurry and without following proper procedures.
- GIDC's land which was originally acquired for industrial purposes has not been allotted for SEZ, which will use land for other purposes as well.
- The strain on natural resources, especially water.

192 Mukta Srivastava, "Statement on Singur", (3 October, 2008). Circular letter to scats@sify.com (3 October, 2008).

193 Interview with Adlin Regina Bai, Pennourmai Iyakkam Office Bearer, Madurai, 2 November, 2008. And M. Shanti, Construction Workers union General Secretary, Madurai, 4 November, 2008.

194 Savio Abrece, " The Struggle Against SEZs in Goa," *Social Action* 58/3 (July-September, 2008): 296-300.

De-notification of SEZ in Goa was the result of relentless pressure from almost the entire state; villagers, educated, middle class, professional, activist, the Church and media.[195]

In Karnataka, at Mangalore, due to the continued struggle of *Krishi Bhoomi Samrakshaka Samiti* (Save Agriculture land organization), the 35,000/- crore Mangalore SEZ project were asked to restrict to only phase I by the expert committee.[196]

In addition to these, though most of the state executives either talk on behalf of the state government and central government or a corporate who wants to set up a factory,[197] there are some opposing voices raised by State Executives.[198]

4.8. Alternative to SEZ

There are some cooperative societies seeking for alternative SEZs, which mainly aimed to address farmers question.

Fertilizer Cooperative (IFFCO) announced that it will set up agriculture-based food processing unit in Nellore in Andrapradesh and make peasants the direct shareholders and it will be named

---

195 Rifat Mumtaz and Madumanti Sardar, "How the SEZ Battle was Won?," *Frontier* 40/36 (March 23- 29, 2008): 7.

196 Sudipto Mondal, "Central Panel Advises Ministry Against manglore SEZ Phase II" *The Hindu*, (Bangalore), 7 March 2008, 4.

197 Chief Secretary of Tamil Nadu speaks on behalf of speak see "Seven IT Majors Show Interest in Gangaikondan SEZ" *The Hindu* (Madurai), 17 March 2008. 5.

198 The Controller and Auditor General of India (CAG) has revealed that government will have Rs.2000/- crore revenue leakage in SEZs. This statement reveals the disturbance of this department with this policy. "Rs.2000-Crore Revenue Leakage in Sezs Units, Says CAG Report", *The Hindu* (Madurai), 12 March 2008, 7.

The Administrative Reforms Commission (ARC) has favored sweeping changes in policy regarding the setting up of SEZs. These include not using prime agriculture land for the purpose and limiting the number of economic zones. And the proportion of land that is permitted to be used by the promoters of SEZs for non-processing activities should be kept to the minimum and the government should encourage SEZ promoted by the farmers. There should be a strict adherence to environmental regulations. Sandeep Joshi, "reforms Commission for Changes in SEZ Policy", *The Hindu* (Madurai), 18 March 2008, 7.

'*Kisan* (Farmer) SEZ'[199] M. S. Swaminathan also suggests starting the same kind of efforts at different places mainly the places where farmers suicide more.

4.9. Development Paradigms and Livelihood

Above discussion invites an argument, which paradigm can solve the livelihood challenges of agrarian communities? Whether it is neo-liberalization which aims to have development through industrialization and promotion of agro-industries or an economy which emphasis the development through agriculture growth aimed for food security and sustainable development? The field study shows the trend of destruction towards livelihood aspects in the SEZ policy, and also other studies regarding different policies related to neo-liberal economic paradigm prove this fact.[200] So, in reality, the expansion of neo-liberal economic development causes the destruction of livelihood base of farmers either through acquirement or environmental degradation. Hence, the claim of political parties on behalf of the farmers can't be right as it does not deal with the core issue. At this juncture, the argument of people's movements for an alternative economy is to be focused and put into operation.

Conclusion

Above discussion on different responses of political parties, trade unions, people's movements and others can be divided generally and specifically. Among the political parties, all the major parties support SEZ at the same time show their slight differences based on their ideological strands.

BJP and RSS seek to address the question of livelihood base of farming communities. At the same time they are for the promotion of export industry. They do not address the contradicting factors with their demands. Though some leaders raise the concern of farmers, it does not come to the forefront.

---

199 "IFFCO to Set up Kisan SEZ" *The Hindu* (Madurai), 4 January 2008. 7.

200 Policies like JNURM, Express Highways etc.,

Congress does not want to shift from their policy, though they show public concern regarding the farmer's questions. Sonia Gandhi's words were never translated into practice.

Left parties mainly seek incorporation of labour law within the SEZ Act. At the same time they raise their concern for the Agriculture labourers and Small farmers all over the country. But CPI (M) failed to take farmer's question into consideration in their ruling states and even used force to implement the SEZ over against the concerns of farmers. However, CPI opposes with CPI (M) in this matter. Among the regional parties, it is difficult to place them in ideological terms.

Politically affiliated trade unions have shown a change in attitude with the change in the ruling party. The Left unions play different roles in States ruled by the Congress or BJP, but connive with the governments in Left-ruled States. Moreover, the trade unions failed to unite together for their cause. The left while they believe in "workers of all lands unite"[201] as suggested by Marx, and have failed to come together. There are occasions when unions have come together "for some struggle" but parted ways as soon as the struggle came to an end. At the same all the trade unions, except INTUC, raised their voices in support of the farmers cause though they have failed to take any sound action.

Indian Federation of Chamber of Commerce and Industry and Confederation of Indian Industry, both never concerned about the livelihood issues of farmers, but only anxious about the regional variation in the so-called development.

The response of People's Movements differ from the political parties and trade unions, they translate their words into action without any compromise in different places with various means. The major difference between the political parties and trade unions is the paradigm of development focused to solve the livelihood question of farming communities.

201 Karl Marx and Fredrick Engels, *Selected Works,* Vol. 3 (Moscow: Progress Publishers, 1976), 177.

Chapter V

Biblical Theological Response to the Challenges of Livelihood

Introduction

Various responses have made from different perspectives against the challenges of SEZ on the livelihood of Agriculture Labourers and Small Farmers. Responses are based on the perception of economic paradigm. This chapter has specific interest to look at these challenges from the biblical-theological understanding, which focuses on an Economy that affirms livelihood.

SEZ is part of an economic development paradigm, i.e., Neo-liberalization, in which the question of livelihood of certain section has been left out, so the assumption of this economy has to be questioned because the Biblical concepts and covenantal understanding assert the livelihood of people. Therefore, this challenge on the question of livelihood is a theological challenge as well as the challenge to the faith community. Thereby, by looking at the biblical understanding of economy, and its characteristics, how can we address the challenges of SEZ on the question of livelihood is the core issue that has been discussed here.

5.1. Biblical Theology

Biblical Theology seeks to clarify themes and ideas encountered in the Bible or in the different books or portions thereof.[202] The themes and ideas encountered in particular contexts, which have continuity and coherence.[203] On the basis of the themes, those have come out from various contexts, brought together here to understand the thrust of biblical theology, especially regarding the economic activity.

5.2. Biblical Theological Understanding of Economy

The understanding of economy is related with daily interaction of people with nature and fellow beings. It starts from the simple institution, i.e., family to complex institution, i.e., state and so on. So, we begin the discussion on economy from the family. The Greek word from which we derive economy is *oikonomia.* It is a compound of *oikos,* which means 'household', and *nomos,* law or management. So, Economy literally means "the law or the management of the Household."[204] The household is connected with the production, distribution, and consumption of the necessities of life. M Douglas Meeks explains household as 'the site of human livelihood.'[205] So this site, i.e., Israel as a household of God, in which Biblical theological concepts emerged and formulated. Therefore, the Biblical Theology is connected with economy.

The concept of 'household' began with the life in totality--in Genesis chapters1 and 2. It is explained as the mutual enrichment of all the creation and can be called as 'Household of God'. The activities

---

202 Alan Richardson, "Biblical Theology", in *A Dictionary of Christian Theology,* ed. by Alan Richardson (Norwich: SCM Press, 1974), 36.

203 Xavier Leon-Dufour, "Introduction: Biblical Theology", in *Dictionary of Biblical Theology,* 2nd Edition, Translated by P. Joseph Cahill (London: Geoffrey Chapman, 1973), xvii.

204 Indukuri John Mohan Razu, *Global Capitalism as Hydra: A New Look at Market, Money and MNC's* (New Delhi: ISPCK, 2006), 267.

205 M. Douglas Seeks, *God The Economist: The Doctrine of God and Political Economy.* 3.

of God's household aimed for the welfare of all human beings. Hence, the economy in the Bible can be called as People's Economy.[206] It has certain characteristics, which have come out from different contexts to teach the people how to practice biblical faith among Israelites. Major characteristics relate with means of production and combining resources with labour in People's economy follow:

5.2.1. The Major Means of Production in Peoples Economy

In any economy 'nature' is the major means of production; it includes land, water, forest etc. Nature provides resources. People's Economy is based on God, people and nature. The relation between these three constitutes People's economy, which is based on biblical theology. It has clear explanation regarding the Ownership, Use, and Distribution of nature and the resources in it. In case the relation between these three gets affected it explains how it is to be restored.

The Bible shows the intrinsic connection between faith and resources of the nature. The faith of Israel began with Abraham's expectation of God's promises, i.e., land. Promised Land and their life in the land have to be related with the covenant; it deals with a way of life, which has staunch egalitarian concept; no accumulation of resources, no slavery, and so on. However, during the monarchic period, with two notable exceptions Hezekiah and Josiah, the very land that promised to create a space for human joy and freedom became the very source of dehumanizing exploitation and oppression. In brief the story of the Bible is the story of people with the land. Thus, the teaching of the Bible relates with the nature and resources in it. Therefore, nature and the resources in it are not just property but it is a full enactment and embodiment of God's will for the earth.[207] Thus, the characteristics of people's economy are based on the covenantal understanding of the faith community.

---

206 It is not an economy in which human being is at the centre, but the economy which focuses the livelihood question of human being at the core, and it keeps a precondition that enrichment of life in totality can only bring livelihood to all.

207 Bruce C. Brich, Walter Brueggemann and et.al, *A Theological Introduction to Old Testament* (Nashville: Abingdon Press, 1999), 175-176.

According to Crusemann, "the Book of covenant (Torah) presumes an agricultural society."[208] Everyday life relationships of agrarian communities' have been addressed in the Book of covenant. Therefore, it has definite teaching on nature and resources in it; land, water etc., control, use, and distribution. The major teaching with regard to resources, i.e., Land, water and forest, follow:

5.2.1.1. Control over Resources

5.2.1.1.1. The concepts 'Land' and 'Earth'

The two words 'Land' and 'Earth' are used in the Bible. The word 'earth' carries the meaning of all nature and 'Land' is part of this nature. The example shows regarding the use of land in reference with the Israelites is a model for all the people in the earth. Some of the explanation regarding land and earth follow:

According to Walter Bruggemann, the Bible concerns God's foundational gift of the earth. The Hebrew word '*erets*' means earth, which belongs to God and may not be denied by God. This word also used for 'land'. The word functions very differently when it is rendered 'land' rather than 'earth'. 'Land' as contrasted with 'earth' is always assigned owned, and occupied. When one talks about 'land' everything is owned according to legal legitimation that makes very great difference in social reality and social possibility[209]. However, these differences have to be seen in its deeper meaning, according to Bastian Wilenga:

> "God makes a new beginning with human-on-the-earth (cf. Gen. 12: 1-3), when God calls that one person, Abraham, to go to the '*erets*' (land), which I will show you, in order that 'by you all the families of the '*erets*' (earth) shall bless themselves' (Gen. 12: 1-3). Concentrating on Israel- in the land, it is humankind-on the earth which God is aiming

---

208 Frank Crusemann, *The Torah: Theology and Social History of Old Testament,* (Edinburgh: T & T Clark, 1996).

209 Walter Brueggemann, "The Earth is Lord's-A Theology of Earth and Land," *Sojourner* (October, 1986): 29.

> at. The crucial role of the land in the faith of Israel reminds us that the earth is the aim of God's ways" [210]

The double nature of the land is reflected in other Old Testament. Gerhard Von Rad points out that the term 'heritage' or 'patrimony' (inheritance) which initially designates the defined property of a clan or tribe, is extended in Deuteronomic usage to refer to the 'patrimony of Israel', a term that expresses Israel's right to occupy this land as its own defined property. However, the land is also spoken of as the 'patrimony of Yahweh,' an expression that makes the land a holy land, Yahweh's personal property[211].

5.2.1.1.2. Land Ownership

The Bible affirms that, the creator of whole universe has the sole right upon the land (Lev. 25:1). The land has been given to humankind so that can they use its resources for their livelihood and not for accumulating its benefits for one's own sake. The Bible speaks that human being are the temporary possessor of land for a short stay. Walter Zimmerli comments that:

> "It is also striking that Old Testament recounts two occupations of the land- first, remarkable provisional, in which the patriarchs look forward in hope to the day when the land will really be totally given to their descendents and a second occupation by what it now the people of Israel. The '*P*' *stratum* framed the theological conception for the first phase by speaking of the 'land of sojourning' or land of 'temporary citizenship'. " [212]

Even the faith of Israel means to deny ultimate ownership of resources to any other. This concept of faith is against every imperialistic, monopolistic, and exploitative power. This claim finds

---

210 Bastian Wilenga, *It's a Long Road to Freedom-Perspectives of Biblical Theology* (Madurai: TTS, 1986), 139.

211 Walter Zimmerli, *Old Testament Theology in Outline* (Edinburgh: T&T. Clark Ltd., 1978), 66.

212 Ibid., 65.

intolerable of other claims such as those made by Pharaoh who said "My Nile is My Own; I made it..." (Ezek. 29:3).

Walter Brueggemann points out the three task set by the Torah for land management, which is based on the absolute ownership of God:

> "The first is prohibition of images... Images refer to making controllable representations of our best loyalties and visions. They are efforts to reduce to manageable and predictable form the sources of value and power in our lives.... (thus) when the land is fully controlled, it is easy to imagine that the land has been generated by the community and can be used for its own objectives." (Deut. 8:7)
>
> "The second task of landed Israel is to keep Sabbath.... it is a central affirmation to Israel about the character of life and land as gift. It is the institutional reminder to Israel that cessation from frantic activity will not cause the world to disintegrate or society to collapse.... Land Sabbath is a reminder that; land is not from us but is a gift to us, land is not fully given over to our satiation....Debt Sabbath (Deut. 15: 1-11) is a dramatic affirmation that human society does not rest finally on buying and selling, owning and collecting. Landed people are accustomed to managing things. And as we mange things we would manage people. We manage them by taxation and interest rates, by debts and mortgages and soon everyone is either owner of theirs or part of the owned....(but) Sabbath in Israel is the affirmation that people like land cannot be finally owned or managed"
>
> Thirdly, "land is for sharing with all the heirs of the covenant even those who have no power to claim it."[213]

Thus, the People's Economy, which is based on biblical theology negates the absolute ownership of human being over resources, i.e., land, water etc.,. The ownership of human being over resources

213 Walter Brueggemann, *The Land*, 62-67.

is relative and it is based on the need of the people. Some of the natures of this ownership follow:

- Resource Ownership as Inheritance: The Bible speaks of land as inheritance of the people of Israel. There are two terms used in the Bible to note inheritance; '*nahala*'[214] (inheritance) and '*Ahuzza*'[215] (Property/possession). According to Fridrich Horst, the two themes are essentially same. The term '*Ahuzza*' is an abstract juridical term compared to more general term '*nahala*'. In most cases, the two terms are used together. '*Nahala*' is the ownership of the land as passed down from father to son.[216] In the pre-monarchial period of Israel's history the economic life was embedded in the family and clan relationship on the social level. Access to the land and other related resources were based on these relationships.[217] This 'inheritance' concept exercised in the 'site of human livelihood'.

The land possessed through inheritance is inalienable and retains the right for its redemption in the year of jubilee. In most cases the land possessed as inheritance, ancestral property is never given out for sale (cf.1 Kgs. 21.3ff.). The prophets vehemently protested the commoditization of the land (Isa. 5:8; Mic. 2:1ff.).[218]

* Ownership of Resources: A Sign of Freedom and Identity: The land in the Bible is a sign of freedom and identity. There is no entity for a community or a people without the role of land. In Gen.4: 9-13, when Cain is expelled from the land he becomes rootless and Godless. He became a man without security. Same way, when Israelites

---

214 Num. 18:23; 16:6; Josu. 13:23: Ruth 4:6.

215 Gen. 47:11; 17:8; Lev. 14:34.

216 Ruide Menzes, "The Pentateuchal Theology of Land," *Bible Bhashyam* (March, 1986): 5.

217 R. Alberty, *History of Israelite Religion*, Vol. I (London: SCM Press, 1994)

218 Yahgkahao Vashum, "Theology of Land: A Naga Perspective," *The Tribal Worldview and Ecology*, ed. by A Wati Longcher and Yahgkahao Vashum (Jorhat: The Tribal Study Centre, 1998), 80.

were taken captives to the foreign land they become rootless and their identity as free nation was shattered.[219] This understanding explains that the people's identity and means of production go together.

- Resource Ownership Holdings: In the biblical tradition no absolute model is propagated regarding the holding ownership; whether it is public or private? Larger or small? But, by understanding the basic perspective of the God, who hears the cries of creation and thus sustains the life of all and also by looking at the ban of interest, which is to prevent a threat of life by taking away resources as debt payment, one can perceive the teaching of the Bible. Biblical theology never encourage accumulation of land (Deut. 17: 14-20) at the same time never discourage to keep the small property[220] (1 Kgs. 21.3ff.).

Church Fathers in principle held to the Biblical approach. In their understanding, explained by Ulrich Duchrow, "what is not common property anyway should be private property by relative right so that it can be to the benefit of all. On no account must it be misused for private wealth accumulation."[221]

5.2.1.2. Resource Management

Biblical theology explains the fact that when the landless people became landed people, the need for having new institution has required. Walter suggests two models of Land management in the history of Israel; Pre-Kingship period and Kingship period.

Pre-Kingship period judges who intervened primarily during the crisis. Though it was not effective and not disciplined it has strong egalitarian values. But during the Kingship period, they were

219 Yahgkahao Vashum, "Theology of Land: A Naga Perspective," *The Tribal Worldview and Ecology*, ed. by A Wati Longcher and Yahgkahao Vashum (Jorhat: The Tribal Study Centre, 1998), 86.

220 Edward Dommen, *How Just is the Market Economy* (Geneva: WCC Pub., 2003), 53.

221 Ulrich Duchrow, *Property for People not for Profit* (London: Zed Books, 1988), 164.

supposed to be different (Deut. 17: 14-20) from their surrounding nations and kingship system, which operate accumulative manner and considered resources as possessions.

The model of land management offered in Deut. 17:14-20 consists of three parts: first, permission is given to have a King but demanding limits are set on his character: "one from among your brethren you shall set as King over you…" (Deut. 14-15)

Walter Brueggemann says this contrast is clear and sharp, "the issue is not pure blood or tribal connection but that the land must be managed by someone nurtured in the understanding and memories of Israel."[222] He further adds that,

> "'One from the brethren' means one in the context of covenant, one whose discernment of power gifts and tasks…this teaching thus calls for a radical redefinition of what kingship is all about. It is not to control the land but to enhance the land for the sake of covenant partners to whom the King is bound by common loyalties and memories"[223]

In vv.16-17 three things added; he (King) must not multiply horses (Military Power), multiply wives[224] (Foreign Policy), Gold and silver (Economic Expansion). The integrating aspects of economic, foreign and economic factors in the society well connected in the covenant. Military power on the one side relates with the protection of resources from the outside forces. But, during the Judges' time also timely military interventions were there. It was not institutional and not used for internal coercion. But, nearby countries, who kept Kingship system, followed military power in order to expand resources or for the implementation of tributary system in which they could have control over resources and labour power of people. So, the Kingship system among the Israelites sought here an alternative system. Marrying from other king's daughter was part

222 Walter Brueggemann, *The Land*, 76.

223 Ibid.

224 King Solomon married many wives was part of his foreign policy and alliances (I Kgs. 9:16).

of foreign policy through they could have a mutual control over resources and labour power for their benefits. This policy was in its root itself rejected by giving the command that King must not marry multiply. Accumulation of Gold and Silver is the symbol of economic expansion which would eventually lead Israel into oppressive ways. These institutional practices, which are corresponding to Torah, should obey by the King, otherwise "I (God) will cut off Israel from the Land" (I Kgs. 9:7).

Land resource management is the central fact of Israel's faith. The Kings are not free to manage the land as they wish in Israel. Their very existence as a faith community is in line with the resources management, which is based on the covenant.

5.2.1.3. Resource Use

5.2.1.3.1. Use of Nature and it Resources Based on the Concept "till and keep it"

The Bible speaks the use of nature and it resources; 'till and keep it.' Use for our need, i.e., meant for 'till'. At the same it should be followed by sustainability, i.e., 'keep it'. Unrestricted use of nature and its resources, which results exhaustion of resources is a denial of God's law. The sustainable use of resources is emphasized by giving the 'Sabbath' law; rest to the resources only to keep it (sustainability). 'Till and keep' also emphasizes the mutual relation or association between land and agriculture life of small farmers, who mainly emphasize the need as well as the sustainability of land.

5.2.1.3.2. Use of Resource Based on the Concept "Stewardship"

A steward is defined as a person entrusted with the management of another's property. According to Clare Palmer the term 'steward' in the Bible refers 'to the man (sic) over the house' with responsibility to the master for the affairs of household and its possessions. Wolff comments that, "they (human being) are living icon of God and hence stewards over the world of God; they are 'handiworks' of God (Gen. 2:7) and hence servants and worshippers of God"[225]

225 H. W. Wolff, *Anthropology of the Old Testament* (London: SCM, 1974), 227.

The duty of steward is an assigned duty by his or her master. For human being, God assigned a duty 'fill the earth and subdue it' (Gen. 1:28). The Hebrew word 'abas', which translated as 'subdue', is used to express various ideas as to tread down, to press, to rape (cf. Esth. 7:8; Mic. 7:9), to reduce someone to the status of slave (Neh. 5:5; 2 Chr. 28:10) or to bring nations under subjugation (2 Sam. 8:11).[226]And the 'dominion' Hebrew word '*radah*' means 'to rule', 'to dominate' and 'to exercise power'.

However, Loren Wilkison says that the commands 'subdue' and 'rule' in some sense reversed by the rest of scripture. It first appears in Gen. 2:

> "Here human responsibility is described by two verbs, *abad* and *shamar'* till and keep'. The word *abad* sometimes translated as 'work' or 'serve'. In fact *abad* is the basic Hebrew word for 'serve' or even 'be a slave to'. And the word *shamar* is translated variously 'keep' 'watch' or 'preserve'. The significant thing about the both words is that they describe actions undertaken not primarily for the sake of the doer, but for the sake of the object of the action. The kind of till, which is to be done as a service to the earth. The keeping of garden is not just for human comfort but is a kind of preservation. Thus human ruling should be exercised in such a way as to serve and preserve the beasts, the trees, and the earth itself.[227]

Thus, the term 'dominion' and 'subdue' (Gen 1:28) permit no license for the unbridled exploitation and subjugation of nature.

Wendell Berry uses two terms "exploiter of creation and a nurturer of creation; Exploiters are specialists whose concern is efficiency and whose goal is profit. And nurtures are specialist whose concern is care and whose goal is health -- their own communities and their lands...only in nurturing is there stewardship."[228]

---

226 C. Westermann, *Genesis 1-11* (London: SPCK, 1984), 759.

227 Loren Wilkinson, *Earth Keeping: Christian Stewardship of Natural Resources* (Michigan: William B. Eerdamans Publishing Company, 1989), 209.

228 Wendbell Berry, *The unsettling of America* (San Francisco: Sierra Club Books, 1977), 7. Quoted in Fred Van Dyke and et.al, *Redeeming Creation: The Biblical*

Douglas John Hall, in his book, *Imaging God: Dominion as Stewardship* explains the image of God is that something which we do. "It is not substantial, but relational: it describes our unique calling to be in responsible relationship with God, with each other and with the rest of the creation"[229]. Thus, the understanding of 'dominion' is to understand in relation to the caring action of God[230] towards the creation.

Though the concept "stewardship" has slightly been criticized by some Indian theologians[231], the synonymous of this word has been used in many of Jesus' parables to show the responsibility of human being in relation to his fellow beings.

Gandhi explains the concept of 'trusteeship'; it indicates the idea 'stewardship'. Those who owned resources should be trustee of wealth for service. However, his understanding of 'trusteeship' in the context, where caste system prevails, should be criticized.

5.2.2. Combining Labour with Resources in People's Economy

People's Economy, based on biblical theology, explains the significant factors that are to be kept while combining the resources and labour. Thus, it gives a welfare measures for labour. The faith of Israelites relates with this understanding.

5.2.2.1. Work for All: It Rejects Division of Labour

In a biblical view, labour or work is an essential part of human life even in paradise. The First mission has given to human being is that "till and keep" the land (Gen. 2: 15). In Exodus, it is part of God's commandment (Ex. 20: 9). The power to 'dominion' and 'subdue' the resources specifies his/her vocation. It has given to fulfill human being's vocation, which goes in line with the commandments of

---

Basis of Environmental Stewardship (Illinois: Intervarsity Press, 1996), 140.

229 Loren Wilkinson, *Earth Keeping in the 90's: Stewardship of Creation* (Michigan: William B. Eerdamans Publishing Company, 1980), 285-86.

230 See more explanation under the topic 'Labour as Ministry in relation to nature' in this chapter.

231 George Mathew Nalunnakkal, *Green Liberation: Towards An Integral Eco-Theology* (New Delhi: ISPCK, 1999), 256-261.

God. Thus, vocation is defined by human being's service to God.[232] It means service to fellow beings as well as all nature.

Apostle Paul emphasizes that no one should live at the expenses of others[233] (Acts. 20:34; 2 Thess. 3: 7-9). Thus, People's economy emphasizes the work for all. But, neo-liberal economic paradigm does divide the workers and push certain section under deprivation.

5.2.2.2. Labour as the means of life: Right to adequate wage

For the survival of humanity as well as for the protection of nature, labour is essential. So, labour can be called as labour, only then it becomes a constructive or protective practice of human being. In people's economy, it is the means of life for human being and the protection of life, in general. However, the disharmony between the labour and fruit occurs (Gen. 3: 18). It is the outcome of greed.[234] But, labour is not cursed but the soil. (Gen. 3:17). Though there is a bitter disharmony between effort and fruit, once more labour is part of life. People economy seeks to practice biblical vision of a future in which 'they shall not labour in vain' (Isa. 65:23, RSV), it indicates the situation where there will be perfect harmony between effort and fruit.[235]

However, neo-liberal economic paradigm expands the disharmony between labour and fruit. Those who are having labour power do not have right over fruits. Instead, their labour power is being exploited. It also destroys the elements of people's economy by forcefully acquiring the land and destroying the rural life where labour consistent with his/her skill.

---

232 John H. Stek, "Salvation, Justice, and Liberation in the Old Testament," *Calvin Theological Journal* 13/2 (November, 1978): 137.

233 During the time of church fathers, the Greeks and Romans considered labor-related activities were degrading. A free human being was supposed to engage in ethical, philosophical and political activities. True citizens ought not to work. The church fathers went against the tide, emphasizing like Paul that idleness is wrong and it is linked with exploitation others.

234 The greed for more or more than human being required consuming, Adam and Eve were allowed to take all the fruits except the few but the greed to have more ended up in failure, results the disharmony between God and Human being. (Gen. 2)

235 Bastian Wilenga, *Biblical Perspective on labour,* (TTS: Madurai, 1982), 35-36.

5.2.2.3. Labour as Ministry in Relation to Nature

The creation story of the Bible says, Human being is formed from the dust of the field "Adam" from "Adamah". It shows that man and land belong together. And he was put to Eden Garden, as in Gen. 2: 15, to 'till and keep' it. The word for tilling "abad" means to work or to "serve." According to Bastian Wilenga, these words should read in line with notion of 'dominion over nature' which is used in Gen. 1:26[236]. It meant that ruling over nature has strong connotation of protecting the nature.

The understanding of dominion relates with the understanding that human labour reflects 'Image of God'. Biblical accounts begin with the very nature of God, i.e., the creator who works, and create us in his own "image and likeness". This image of God establishes kinship between humankind and God. According to Von Rad it would seem that the Kingship between God and humans implied in the phrase 'image of God' must be understood in terms of shared function[237]. According to J.G.F. Collison biblical way of expressing this shared function lies in the command to "fill the earth and subdue it" and "till the garden and keep it". He further says that, God, who is always the efficient cause, adopts human being as instrument cause. Thus, God intends humans to be instrument for fulfilling his sovereignty over creation. But, human being failed to prove themselves as an adequate instrumental cause. Eventually nature being corrupted, the antagonism between nature and humans emerged and frustration of nature also took place. [238] So, the cosmic redemption is possible only through knowing and keeping the instrumental cause properly. It is by knowing the role of human as an 'image of God.'

So, the concept of 'labour' can understand in relation to the knowledge that we are 'image of god' with certain responsibilities. John H. Stek opines that, "As God's sovereign creative work…led to rest, so the work of God's image bearers done in God's good creation

236 Bastian Wilenga, *Biblical Perspective on Labour,* (TTS: Madurai, 1982), 34.

237 G. Von Rod, *Old Testament Theology,* Vol.1 (London: Olive Boyd, 1962), 144-17.

238 J. G. F. Collision, "Biblical Perspectives on Stewardship of Earth's Resources," *Bangalore Theological Forum* 18/4 (October-December, 1986): 157.

and in God's service would lead to rest."[239] This understanding equally helps one to know the Other (God) Labour[240]; redemptive labour (Josh. 24: 31), other labour (labor of Fellow human being), and labour in totality (production process in the nature).

The division of labour is the result of self ignorance,[241] i.e., forgetting the fact that we are image of God. Self-ignorance causes dejection of oneself as well as rejection of others and their actions. Eventually one fails to understand oneself and co-creatures, and all their actions.

In human history, division of labour has increased more and more with the passage of time. Consequently, not only labour has been divided and forced to look down as an inferior worker but also certain groups of the society have been pushed to more insecure and vulnerable work conditions where there is no assurance of their security. Labour has been commoditized; as a result labour or work is covered with image of money. It challenges the biblical concept 'image of God' and human labour which reflects its very nature.

The People's Economy highlights the concept 'image of God' over against the dominant economy, which seeks maximum production at the cost of nature and labour power. The most significant sections in the society, who protect the nature, are Small Farmers and Agriculture Labourers. They live in the land, protect the top soil and uses the sustainable methodologies to yield production.

5.2.2.4. Labour is to be Protected- Social security should be ensured

Labour is to enrich life of oneself and fellow being. So, it is to be protected with efficacious law, as it is a biblical command. God's declaration of Sabbath itself shows this factor emphatically. Giving rest to the laborers is the significant part of the commandment. 'Sabbath' law is to protect the life of the producers; labourers, land,

239 John H. Stek, op. cit., 135.

240 M. Douglas Meeks explains regarding God work as Trinitarian work in which each person of Trinity engages in "distinctive personal work", "corporate work", "equalitarian work" see more M. Douglas Seeks, op.cit., 132-34.

241 The state in which we forget ourselves as image of God, or false conception of image of God.

and animals, In brief, Sabbath is the first labour law God instituted for His/Her own very nature, i.e., 'work',[242] and also for all the working class. The labour law which has instituted by God has been undermined in SEZ. This law relates with time span of labour.

When Jews followed God-instituted labour law, Roman writers complained it as a weekly day of strike. Bastian Wilenga says "throughout the centuries this celebration (celebration of Sabbath) has been a quiet, joyous protest against the takers of time, the exploiters,"[243] and he further adds that the manna tradition (P tradition, Exod. 16: 4-5; 22-30) affirms the fact that the workers should receive pay also for a weekly day off-- sixth day provides bread for two days.[244]

Therefore, the alienation and exploitation of labour endanger enrichment of life and cause the breaking of commandment. Labour efforts and work should be used for sustainable production, not for accumulation. Restoration of labourers' health and life is part of enriching life in totality.

5.2.3. Distribution or Claims of Production

The Peoples economy gives a detailed picture on distribution of resources as well as claim on production. Claim over production can be settled through the distribution of resources. The role of people is significant in this process. So, distribution of land in Josh. 14:5 and 19:49 suggests or implies a form of the tradition in which allotment or distribution of land was determined by the people at large rather than by Joshua[245]. According to Norman K. Gottwald, the meaning of allotment or distribution meant that "all tribes found a home in

---

242 Ex. 20: 8-11, priestly tradition explains the "work' of YAHWH and 'rest' of YAHWH. It has presented over against the understanding of Mesopotamian culture and religion, there the gods were considered as Supreme Being who were enjoying leisure, whereas human being carried the burden of labour. And those human beings who manage to escape from the toil are almost divine, like the kings. In Gen. 1, priestly tradition rejected this understanding. See more Bastian Wilenga, *Biblical Perspective* ..., 51.

243 Ibid., 49.

244 Ibid.

245 Norman K. Gottwald, op. cit., 183.

the land and settled down to a life of autonomous economic self development based on their land holding".[246] This biblical model shows that no one can accumulate more. Thus, peoples economy is a need based economy. This idea can be seen with 'manna tradition', which never promotes want-based economy. Also, it is confirmed by Jesus prayer in which daily need is the centre of prayer.

5.2.3.1. Resource Restoration: Claim over Means of Production

The tribes of Israel that settled in the promised land of Palestine started to practice more or less equal distribution of the land among the families. But, inevitably inequalities developed. For one reason or other, people got indebted had to work as bonded labourers and even lost their lands. If nothing is done against such unnatural developments, the rich would grow richer and poor would grow poor. Israel tried to prevent such drift to inequality and the injustice and slavery which result from it. One such institution was that of "redemption',[247] it is based on the law of 'Sabbath' and 'Jubilee year' in the holiness code. Redeeming the fellow Israelites, who loss relative right over the resources and thereby claims on production should be resorted. It is the duty of Israelite. Thus, the chief content of the direction for the year of Jubilee, the restoration of land ownership right, naturally presupposes that Israel already settled in civilized conditions on the land but only assumes this to have already taken place and might go back into the early period of Israel's settlement. [248].

In brief, we can conclude that, nature and resources in it belong to God, and we have only relative ownership, that also must be exercised with regard to God's covenant. Covenant uphold God's justice to all, and extend relative right over resources for all the creatures.

246 Norman K. Gottwald, op. cit., 183.

247 Ibid.

248 Martin Noth, *Leviticus* (London: SCM Press, 1965), 185; Indukuri John Mohan Razu, op. cit., 275-78.

5.3. Biblical Theological Understanding of Economy: A Challenge to the Livelihood Challenging Forces

The covenantal understanding has been questioned by the practices of Israelites. There are some vocations, prophets condemned the Israelites, who went away from the covenantal understanding of resources and challenged the livelihood of the poor.

5.3.1. Condemnation: As a Prophetic Voice

According to Walter Wink, "the visible peculiarity of Israel includes an additional component in the apparatus of her governance, namely, the prophet".[249] Prophets are foretellers as well as forth tellers. Most of the Prophets in the Biblical period were forth tellers; they made visible the God's covenant to people as well as the rulers. They read the 'signs of the time' and told the crisis condition and possible remedy for it. They usually stood against the political power, when the political power disregarded above discussed covenant based land management. The presence of Prophet in Israel caused problem to the Kings who followed consumerist ways of life and negated the rights of the common people.

Remarkably, the prophetic entry related with land is articulated in Deuteronomy (Deut. 18:9-22) "when you come into the land… the Lord your God will raise up for you a prophet" and s/he is intended precisely for speech; in the land, in the face of the King, against the idolatrous forms of self-securing[250].

During the Kinship period, the history of Israel presented as, according to Walter Wink, a tension between 'royally secured land' and 'covenanted precarious land.'[251] This tension is evident in the prophetic condemnation on behalf of the latter one. Some examples are:

- "Thus says the Lord: 'Have you killed and also taken possession?" (I Kgs. 21:19, RSV)

249 Cited in Bastian Wilenga, *Biblical Perspective on labour,* 90.

250 Ibid., 91-92.

251 Ibid., 100.

Among the 9th Century Prophets, Prophet Elijah made a powerful condemnation (cf. 1 Kgs. 21:1ff) against the King Ahab (Political structure) who sought after Naboth's vineyard (subsistence farmer's resource base) in order to make a vegetable garden for the King. King Ahab regarded land as tradable commodity "...I will give its value in money" (v. 2), in contrast for Naboth Land is not a tradable commodity, but an inalienable inheritance. "The Lord forbid that I should give you the inheritance of my father's...I will not give you the inheritance of my father's." (v. 3). The exchange between the Political Power and Subsistence Farmer expresses two views of land. Walter comments that "Naboth represents traditional covenantal language in which land is not owned in a way that permits its disposal" in contrast to that King "...thinks everything is to be bought and sold and traded and conquered". King's demand was strengthened by the intervention of Jezebel (vv. 4-7) who follows the tradition of Canaanite Kingship system which allows ruling and manipulating through mercantile system. It was alien to Israelites. For Israelites, Kingship is to protect common people. In contrast to that, Jezebel followed the protection of King's interest over against common people's interest. And she used covenant for her own ends (Exod. 22:28) and eventually through wicked way Naboth's life had been taken and his land has been acquired by the King.

However, in v. 17 Elijah as a spokesman of Yahweh appeared against King (Political structure), who manipulated Torah for their own ends and through injustice way taken the land of a farmer. There is first question of indictment "'Thus says the Lord: 'Have you killed and also taken possession?'" (v.19). The Hebrew word used for possess is *yaras*, which has the double meaning 'possess' and 'dispossess'. It is important here such possession only when another dispossessed[252]. He pronounced God's judgment against them. Because they failed to understand the relation between Naboth and Land.

- "Woe to those who devise wickedness...they covet fields, and seize them; and houses, and taken them away; they

252 Walter Brueggemann, *The Land*, 96.

> oppress a man and his house, a man and his inheritance." (Mic. 2:1-3, RSV)

All the 8th century prophets uplift the covenant over against the accumulative practices of the rich class, which deprived the situation of small property holders, the landless, aliens, and widows.

Micah paints a situation where capital owners are eager to seize the fields and houses of their fellow-country folk, eager to oppress people and their inheritance[253]. It was the result of merchant economy and wider use of money. Eventually, the separation between rich and poor had been broadened. Unethical merchant were able to increase their profits. Small peasantry who suffered most in this period, according to Ralph L. Smith, Micah condemns the offenders:

> "The chief offenders were a relatively small group of greedy, powerful business men who spent their nights devising schemes to get possession of the land of the small peasants. The next day they carry out their schemes because they had sufficient economic, political and judicial power to accomplish their goals. Even when their goals deprived a man and his household of their inheritance which was part of covenant right"[254]

Micah condemned the 'doers' or 'planners' of the wickedness

- "...thus says the Lord 'I am speaking in my hot...against all Edom, who with wholehearted joy and utter contempt took my land as their possession because it pasture to plunder it." (Ezek. 36: 5, RSV)

Prophet Ezekiel condemns Edom on the basis of the covenantal understanding. It proclaims the fact the covenantal understanding is universal. It has to be practiced by all nations. It is the mission of the prophet to contempt the activity of Edom who claimed ownership of

253 See more Klaus Koch, *From Amos to Jesus: Biblical Eschatology and Its Social and Political Implications* (Delhi: ISPCK, 1999), 4-5.

254 Ralph L. Smith, "Micah-Malachi", *Word Biblical Commentary* (Texas: Word Book Publishers, 1984), 24-25.

land. The absolute claim of the ownership of land relates with their action that they insulted the landless Israelites. (v.6)

The prophets are the upholders of biblical covenant, which speaks against the life negating factors.

5.3.2. People's Economy: A Challenge to SEZ

Above discussion has given a picture that the resources ownership, use, distribution, mainly is to protect the livelihood of all, and also protection of labour aimed for the same cause. According to Duchrow, the biblical theological practices considered as counter-cultural practices. The dominant cultures of so-called Ancient Near Eastern were based on the absolute ownership over resources, and related to that dominion over labour power.[255]

The economic activities based biblical theology, which named as People's Economy, challenges the economic practices that negate the livelihood of all. Therefore, the challenge of SEZ on the livelihood is a big challenge to the understanding of biblical theology, it is mainly because:

- As People's Economy respects the relative right over small resource holdings, it condemns SEZ. SEZ forcefully changes the ownership of resources from the hands of small farmers to big corporate. And also natural resources holder become capital resources holder, it works on the basis of the law of mammon, which negates God, the absolute owner of resources.
- SEZ removes a major chunk of labour force from skilled to unskilled, from the safe zone to unsafe zone, where they are forced to work for their survival in hazardous condition. The major percentage of the fruit of their labour power goes to the dominant class. Thus, implementation of SEZ negates 'labour' or 'work', which is actually is a sign of God's image--negation of God him/herself. So, people's economy which respects labour with protective measures condemns SEZ.

255 See more Ulrich Duchrow, op. cit., 5-28.

- As People's Economy outlines a use pattern of resources based on biblical theology, it condemns the abuse of land. SEZ is an abuse of land because of unrestricted extraction of water from the land, deforestation of land for setting up Zone, uncontrolled way of setting concrete buildings as infrastructure, dumping the possible hazardous chemical from the production area, and taking away the agriculture land from the people land. In addition, as it has no covenantal law like Sabbath (no environmental law) or concept like 'till and keep the land' (taking Agriculture land away from its protectors; farmers).
- SEZ is based on greed (more production), mainly for foreign exchange. It emphasizes exchange value rather than need value. On the basis of 'manna tradition' People's Economy never supports this view.
- SEZ follows hierarchical strategy in which few enjoy the holdings of land over against the majority. Few share the profit. People Economy based on biblical theology counters this understanding with the concept of 'jubilee year'.
- People's Economy condemns the economic policies which influence adversely the livelihood condition of Agricultures Labourers and Small Farmers. They are being pushed away from the service of God to service of mammon (Agriculture Labour to industrial labour, which is aimed to expand capital); Agricultures and Small farmers generation to generation engaged in agriculture which provides them livelihood. The SEZ policy pushed them to the market economy which exhausts the resources as well as their livelihood.

5.3.3. Prophetic Participation of the Church

The role of the church in the context where biblical covenant is undermined is prophetic. The prophetic participation of the church in the society is well understood by the apostolic tradition. Church, as a community, is called out to participate in rebuilding the society in line with the values of Kingdom of God. Wherever Kingdom values are being undermined those are to be challenged through prophetical voice. So, participating with prophetic voice as well as becoming prophetic voice is the Salvific mission of the church.

The 'salvation' concept in the Bible is based on one's redemption and restoration as well as the role of the redeemer. The concepts 'redemption' and 'restoration' emerged in the socio-economic context of Israel. It is an act exercised by an Israelite for other Israelite who lost resources and related to that livelihood. In the NT the message of cross is the sign of redemption and one who accept the cross message receive restoration. The message of cross demonstrates the hope of restoration or redemption against the life negating factors. So, the faith in 'cross and resurrection' reminds the church to uphold the 'life' over against the evils of death. This understanding calls the church for the prophetic participation against the life negating forces.

Conclusion

Biblical theological understanding shows the factor that the land can't be treated as absolute property. It has to be related with the absolute owner by keeping the relative owner with his/her small holdings. The main aim of resources is for the need of all, not for the accumulation for the sake of few. Same way, labour or work is dignified. It is glorified not for the sake of profit but for enriching the life in totality. The labour and resources, and related production can't be separated. The prophet envisioned this view. So, the community who uphold the biblical covenant has to be challenged the livelihood negating economic activities and seek for alternative economy.

General Conclusion

The policy Special Economic Zone was introduced as part of liberalize move to economy. The main purpose of SEZ was to boost export-oriented growth. The first phase of economic paradigm, i.e., 'Import Substitution Industry' was aimed to protect the domestic industry. During that period enough attention was given to the agriculture sector. However, after one decade, it was shifted towards export orientation. But, at first it was aimed to assist the domestic economy. Later, Indian economy aimed towards economic reforms, it started to undermine all other institutional reforms. Liberalization became the guiding principle of economic policy. External and internal political stand supported and fought for it. It resulted in further liberalization, i.e., under Neo liberalization the Government of India introduced SEZ Act. It carries industry favored laws. To set up SEZ, different kinds of land was acquired and marked for acquiring. Major portion of the land which has been acquired is the livelihood base of agrarian communities. So, the implementation of this policy caused violence and agitations in many places. SEZs set up in many places without having consensus of farmers.

For the agrarian communities, the question of livelihood depends on access to resources either as owner, labour, or tenant. So, land and water is the major livelihood base of these communities. The Agriculture Labourers and Small Farmers constitute the major chunk of farming communities. Thus, the policies related to their livelihood affect these communities. This study has shown that, the various policies of the government related to land affected their livelihood in the past. At present, the implementation of SEZ has also affected their livelihood adversely. It is mainly because they lost their control over natural resources. Consequently most of them were not able to take-care of their livestock and lost income. The compensation which was given to them was inadequate to maintain the same size of land. So, many among them were forced to move towards cities, where they get engaged in unskilled work, contract labour, or causal labour in hazardous condition. Thus, they are forced to be in a place where they are prone to get exploited. Comparatively, they get less income and employment days after setting up Special Economic Zone. Thus, the Neo-liberal economy systematically expands cheap labour market in the so called third world countries with the ardent support of the government, and destroying the domestic economy.

On SEZ, different political parties, trade unions and people's movements have made various responses. Though political parties made statement for the protection of farmers and farming land, they failed to translate that into action. Trade unions failed to come together for the common cause. At the same time people's movements came together and protested against the land acquirement at different places effectively. In most of the places local people came together as group and stood together for the protection of their livelihood base.

The researcher has critically focused on this policy and the economic paradigm which this policy has introduced from a biblical theological perspective. The understanding of economy means literally 'the law or the management of the Household'. The household is connected with the production, distribution, and consumption of the necessities of life. It is 'the site of human livelihood'. It is this site, where Biblical- theological concepts are emerging and formulating. It indicates the intrinsic connection of biblical theology with economy. The insights, we get from biblical concepts regarding the economic activity, depict the people's management of resources. So, the researcher calls it as People's Economy.

The understanding of people's economy based on biblical theology has certain characteristics. It sees the resources as means of life. Human beings only have relative right over it. Thu, it rejects dominant economic paradigm and its very nature: commodization of property, and accumulative ways of holding the resources. According to People's Economy, the management of resources is for the welfare of all, including the creation. Thus, it promotes a sustainable development. Human labour, when it combines with resources; labour has to be protected and should not be divided. Labour law is the primary concern of people's economy. Negation of this basic understanding is a challenge to the community who uphold the biblical covenant.

Therefore,

- The livelihood negating economic policy, i.e., SEZ is to be condemned. Condemnation is a prophetic voice, so Church should either participate with the prophetic voices in the society or become a prophetic voice.
- Opposing the livelihood negation is part of Salvific mission of the church. Salvation carries the meaning of restoration of our fellow being from the depressed condition, in which he/she lost access to resources.
- The Church is called to reject the livelihood negating economic policies and uphold the livelihood asserting economic policies.

So, seeking alternative economy in this context is part of church's mission.

Appendix - 1

Copy of the Schedule -1

Cluster A1

Purpose of this cluster is to know the process and procedures of land acquirement

Sources of Information:
1. Assistant Development Commissioner
2. Village Chief
3. Local Politician
4. Village/ Block officer

Name:
Category:

A1.1. How many acres of land are used for growing crops?
A1.1.1. How many acres of land are used as grazing animals?
A1.1.2. How many acres of land consist of water bodies like Lakes, water tanks, or Ponds?
A1.2. How many acres of land cover SEZ area?
A1.2.1. Out of this how many acres of land are private and common?

A1.3 How did authorities acquire land?
Either was it through rumor or information?
Either was it through using force or persuasion?

A1.4. Did Developers give any promises?
What were they?
Whether promises are fulfilled or not?

A 2

Purpose is to collect information from the locals regarding the procedure

Sources of Information: Villagers, local Politicians, Village chief

Name:
Category:
Village:

A2.1. What was the immediate response of the people, when they heard that their land is going to be acquired?

A2.2. After the announcement of acquisition of the land for SEZ how many months did the villagers have to make necessary arrangement?

A2.3. Did you receive compensation?

A2.4. What was the nature and criteria to get compensation? And how much?

A2.5. Who bargained on behalf of the people to get compensation?

A2.6. Did the developers give any promises?
What were they?

A2.7. Do you (villagers) get any promises given by the developers?

Cluster B

Purpose is to know the condition of livelihood (before and after setting up SEZ)

Sources of information: Market Oriented Farmers, Subsistence Farmers

Name:
Category:
Village:

B (a)1.1. How many acres of Land did/do you have before and after setting up SEZ?

B (a)1.2. What was the approximate income from the land?
- What is the approximate income from the land?

More-
No Change-
Less-

B (a)1.3. Was water available before the SEZ?
B (a)1.4. Is it available now?

More-
No Change-
Less-

B (a)1.5 What was the approximate income from the livestock?
B (a)1.6. What is the approximate income from the livestock?

More-
No Change-
Less-

Cluster **B (b)**

Purpose is to know difference in wage and skill of Laboures

Sources of Information: Subsistence Farmers and Agriculture Laboures

Name:
Category:
Village:

B (b)1.1. How many days of employment do you have?
- Before losing your land
- After losing your land

More-
No Change-
Less-

B (b)1.2. What was the daily wage?
B (b)1.3. What is the daily wage?
More-
No Change-
Less-
B (b)1.4. Did the work you did give you more skills?
More-
No Change-
Less-

Cluster C

Purpose is to know condition of livelihood mainly by comparing the cost of living in relation to the basic necessities of life

Sources information: Subsistence Farmers and Agriculture Laboures, and Market oriented farmers

Name:

Category:

Village:

C1.1. Did you own house before setting up SEZ?
- Do you own house after setting up SEZ?
More- No Change- Less-
- if it is rented one, what is/was rent?
More- No Change- Less-

C1.2. Was your children's school close to your house or village?
- Is your children's school close to your house or village?
More- No Change- Less-

C1.3. Whether the school was private or public?
- Whether the school is private or public?
More- No Change- Less-

C1.4. How much was fee?
- How much is fee?
More- No Change- Less-

C2.1. Did you have any clinic or hospital facility near your house?

- Do you have any clinic or hospital facility near your house?
  More- No Change- Less-
- Was it private or Public?
- Is it private or public?
  More- No Change- Less-

C2.2. What sort of health problems, if any, were you facing?

- What sort of health problems, if any, are you facing?
  More- No Change- Less-

C2.3 What sort of meals did your family eat?

- What sort of meals does your family eat?
  More- No Change- Less-
- Where did you get grains and pulses?
- Where do you get grains and pulses?
  More- No Change- Less-

Copy of the Schedule: 2

Cluster A- Basic Information of SEZ at Madurai Zone (Sivaraikottai)

A.1. To Know the present status of the Land

Source of Information

- Village president
- Official records
- Market-oriented farmer
- Small/marginal farmer
- Agriculture labour

A1.1. How many acres of land are used for growing crops in this village?

A1.2. How many acres of land are used as grazing animals in this village?

A1.3. How many acres of land consist of water bodies like Lakes, water tanks, or Ponds?

A.1.4. How many acres of land may approximately cover SEZ area in this village?

A.1.5. Out of this how many acres of land are private and common?

A.2. To Know the information and response of people regarding the process of SEZ

- Village president
- Market-oriented farmer
- Small/marginal farmer
- Agriculture labour

A2.1. Do you receive proper information?
A2.2. what is the present market price of the land?

Closure to road..............little far from the road.............. more far from the road...........

A2.3. Do you get any information regarding the compensation? And how much?
A2.4. Who bargain on behalf of the people to get compensation?
A2.5. Is there any struggle at present going on what kind of struggle it is?

Cluster-- Data B: To Know the Possible Livelihood Threat

B.1. To Know the possible influence on the livelihood of small farmers

Source of information: Market oriented Small farmers

Small /Marginal farmers

B 1.1. How many acres of Land do you have now?
B 1.2. What is the approximate monthly income from the land?
B 1.3. Is water available in this land?
B 1.4. How do you think, Can you able to purchase same amount of land which can be used for agriculture?
B1.5. What is the approximate income from the livestock?
B1.6. Can you able to maintain the same income after losing your land?

B.2. To Know the possible influence on Agriculture laboures Sources of Information: Agriculture Farmers

B2.1. How many days of employment do you have?
Agriculture
Non-Agriculture

B 2.2. What is the daily wage?
Agriculture
Non-Agriculture

B 2.3. In which work you are skilled more?
Agriculture
Non-Agriculture

Appendix - 2

2.1. MAP OF INDIA

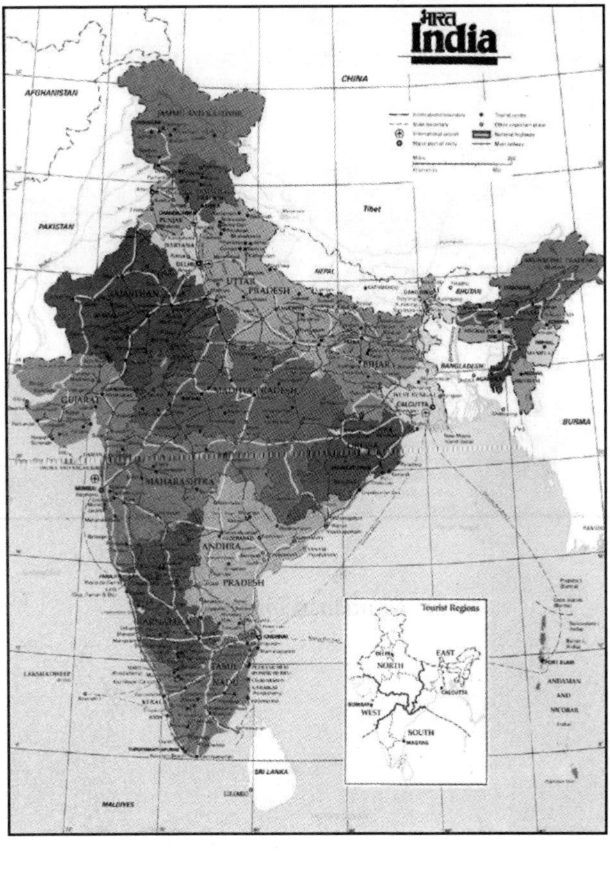

2.2. MAP OF UTTAPRADESH

Mordabad District

2.3. MAP OF MORADABAD

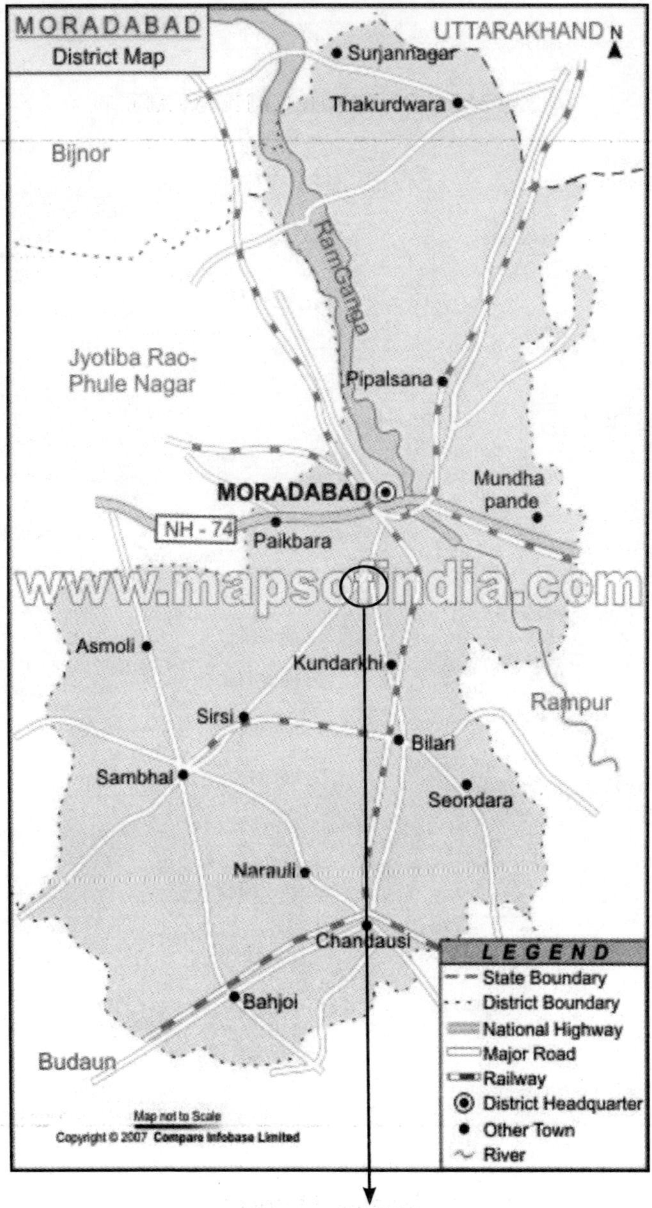

Moradabad Sez Area

2.4. MAP OF TAMILNADU STATE

Madurai District

2.5. MADURAI DISTRICT MAP

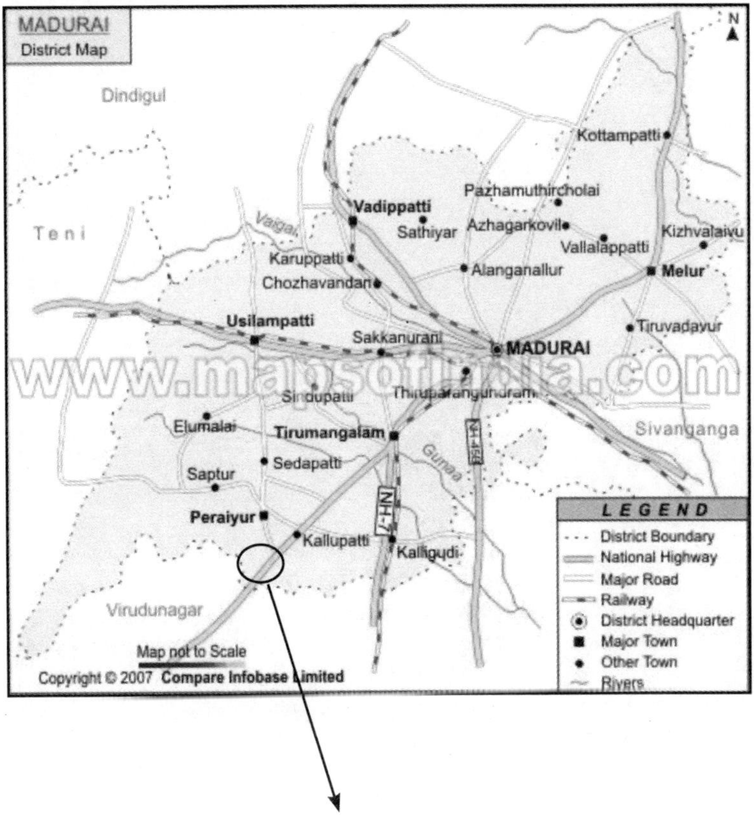

Sivarikottai Village

Appendix - 3

Tables, Charts and Diagram

3.1. Percentage Distribution of Household and Area Owned by Sizes of landholding Class in Rural India in 1953-54, 1961-62 and 1971-72[1]

Size of landholding	*Household*			*Area owned*		
	1953-54	1961-62	1971-72	1953-54	1961-62	1971-72
Marginal (Less than 1ha.)	61.24	60.06	62.62	6.23	7.59	9.76
Small (1.01 to 2.02 ha.)	13.14	15.16	15.49	10.09	12.40	14.68
Semi-medium (2.03 to 4.04)	12.5	12.86	11.94	18.40	20.54	21.92
Medium (4.05 to 10.12 ha.)	9.17	9.07	7.83	29.11	31.32	30.76
Large (10.13 or more ha.)	3.60	2.85	2.12	36.17	28.24	22.91
Total	100	100	100	100	100	100

1 Sources: NSS, 1953-54, 1953-54, 1961-62, and 1971-72 cited in Debal K. Singha Roy, *Peasant Movements in Post-colonial India: Dynamics of Mobilization and Identity* (New Delhi: Sage Pub., 2004), 79.

3.2. Condition of Resources

Category	group	*Condition of the land and income related to it*			*Condition of water*			*Condition of the income from the Livestock*		
		More	*No Change*	*Less*	*More*	*No Change*	*Less*	*More*	*No Change*	*Less*
MF	HT		1				1		1	
	MC			1			1			1
	HJ			2			2		1	1
SF	MC			4			4			4
	HJ			5			5		1	4
AL	MC			4		2	2		3	1
	HJ			3		2	1		3	
Total House-hold	20	0	1	19	0	4	16	0	9	11
Percentage		0%	5.%	95%	0%	20%	80%	0%	45%	55%

Note: Category: MF=Market oriented Farmers, SF= Subsistence Farmers, AL= Agriculture Labourers; Groups: HT= Hindu Takur, MC= Muslim Community, HJ= Hindu Jatav

3.3. Condition of Employment/ labour

Category	*group*	*Condition of Wage (monthly)*			*Condition of Labour Skill*			*Employment days*		
		More	*No Change*	*Less*	*More*	*No Change*	*Less*	*more*	*No change*	*less*
MF	HT	--	1	--	--	1	--		1	
	MC	--		1	---		1		1	
	HJ	--	2	---	---	2	---		2	
SF	MC			4			4			4
	HJ			5			5			5
AL	MC			4			4			4
	HJ			3			3		1	2
Total Household	20	0	3	17	0	3	17		5	15
Percentage	100%	0%	15%	85%	0%	15%	85%	0%	25%	75%

3.4. Condition of housing

Category	*group*	*Condition of housing*		
		Change		*No Change*
		Positive	*Negative*	
MF	HT	-	-	1
	MC	-	-	1
	HJ	-	-	2
SF	MC	-	-	4
	HJ	-	-	5
AL	MC	-	-	3
	HJ	-	-	4
Total	20	0%	-	20
Percentage	100%			100%

3.5. Condition of Education

Category	*group*	*Change of school (private/Public)*			*Change in relation with the distance between home and school*			*Change in relation with the school Fee and transportation expenses*		
		Change		*No Change*	*Change*		*No Change*	*Change*		*No Change*
		Positive	*Negative*		*Positive*	*Negative*		*Positive*	*Negative*	
MF	HT			1			1			1
	MC			1		1			1	
	HJ			2			2			2
SF	MC			4			4			4
	HJ			5			5			5
AL	MC			3			3			3
	HJ			4			4			4
Total Hou-sehold	20									
Percentage		0%	0%	100%		5%	95%	0%	5%	95%

3.6. Condition of Health

Category	group	*Access to hospital/clinic*			*Health Condition*			
		Change		*No Change*	*Change*		*No Change*	*Not Aware*
		Positive	*Negative*		*Positive*	*Negative*		
MF	HT	-	-	1	-	-	1	
	MC	-	-	1	-	-	1	
	HJ	-	-	2	-	-	2	
SF	MC	-	-	4	-	-	2	2
	HJ	-	-	5	-	-	3	2
AL	MC	-	-	3	-	-	2	1
	HJ	-	-	4	-	-	2	2
Total		-	-	20	-	-	13	7
Percentage		0%	0%	100%	0%	0%	65%	35%

3.7. Condition of food habits and source of food items

Category	group	*Condition of food habit*			*Source of food items*		
		Change		*No Change*	*Change*		*No Change*
		Positive	*Negative*		*Positive*	*Negative*	
MF	HT	-		1	-		1
	MC	-		1	-	1	
	HJ	-		2	-		2
SF	MC	-	2	2	-	3	1
	HJ	-	2	3	-	4	1
AL	MC	-	2	1	-	3	
	HJ	-	2	2	-	4	
Total household	20	-	8	12	-	15%	5%
Percentage	100%	0%	40%	60%	0%	75%	25%

3.8. Condition of Livelihood Dependency

Category	*Group*	*Sex*	*Livelihood Dependency*		
			More on Agri.	*More on Non-Agri.*	*Both (Agri & Non-Agri.)*
MF	TR	M	1		
		F	1		
	RR	M	1		
		F	1		
	CS	M	1		
		F	1		
SF	TR	M	1		
		F	1		
	RR	M	1		
		F	1		
	GS	M	1		
		F	1		
AL	PR	M	2		
		F	2		
	CR	M	1		1
		F	2		
Total		20	19		1
Percentage			95%		5%

3.9. Condition of people's Land

Category	*Group*	*Sex*	*Condition of Owing Land*		
			Cultivable In all the seasons	*Seasonal Cultivable*	*Non-cultivable (Waste)*
MF	TR	M		1	
		F		1	
	RR	M		1	
		F		1	
	CS	M		1	
		F		1	
SF	TR	M		1	
		F		1	
	RR	M		1	
		F		1	
	GS	M		1	
		F		1	
AL	PR	M		2	
		F		2	
	CR	M		2	
		F		2	
Total				20	
Percentage				100%	

3.10. Water Availability for Agriculture

Category	Group	SEX	*Availability of Water*				
			No Access	*Seasonal & Access through*			
				well	*tank*	*pond*	*other*
MF	TR	M				1	
		F				1	
	RR	M				1	
		F				1	
	CS	M				1	
		F				1	
SF	TR	M				1	
		F				1	
	RR	M				1	
		F				1	
	GS	M				1	
		F				1	
AL	PR	M				2	
		F				2	
	CR	M				2	
		F				2	
Total		20				20	
Percentage						100%	

3.11. Condition of Wage, Employment days and Skill

Category	group	Sex	*Wage*			*Employment days*			*Condition of Skill*		
			Agri. more	*Non-Agri. more*	*both*	*Agri. more*	*Non-Agri*	*same*	*Agri. more*	*Non-Agri*	*same*
AL	PR	M	2			2			2		
		F	2			2			2		
	CR	M	1		1	1	1		1		1
		F	2			2			2		
Total		8	7	0	1	7	1	0	7	0	1
Percentage			87.5%	0%	12.5%	87.5%	12.5%	0%	87.5%	0%	12.5%

PR= Parayar, CR= Chakliyar,

3.12. People response

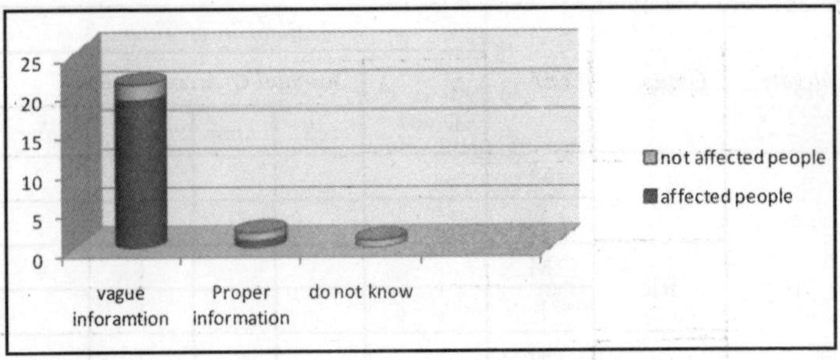

3.13. Employment Growth in EPZ (1966-2002)[2]

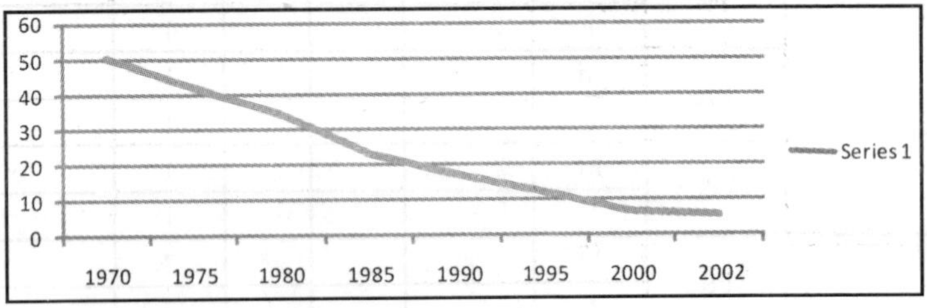

3.14. Average Annual Export Growth (1966-2003)[3]

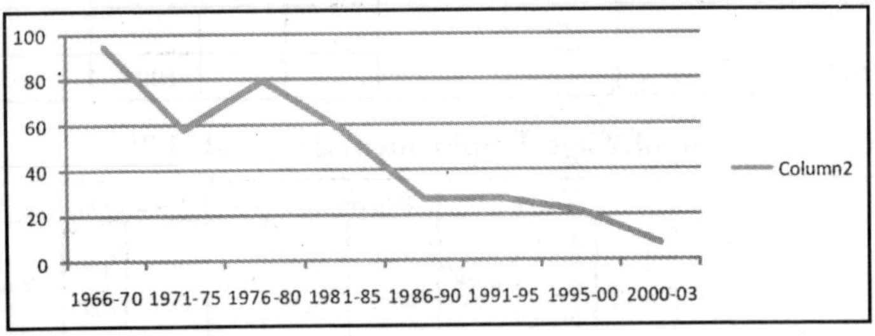

2 Sources: EPZs in India: Analysis of the export performance, ICRIER, New Delhi, 2004

3 Ibid.

3.15. Status of Land in Sivarikootai

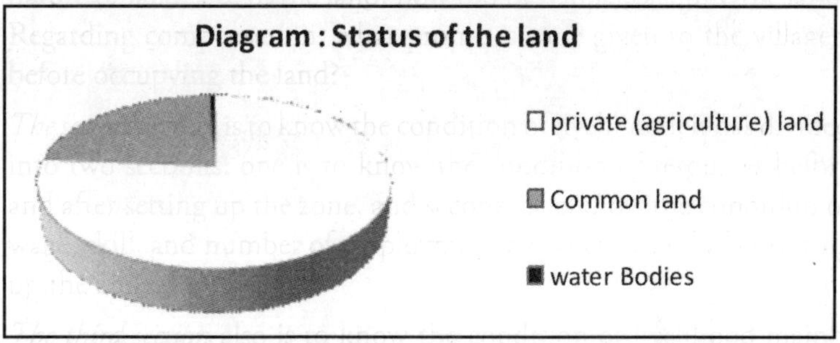

Selected Bibliography

Books

Alberty, R. *History of Israelite Religion*. Vol. I. London: SCM Press, 1994.

Arul Raj, Lawrence G. *Land Reforms.* Madurai: Diwahar Pub., 2001.

Bagchi, Amiya Kumar. "Dialectics of Indian planning From Compromise to Democratic Decentralization and threat of Disarray." In *Industry and Agriculture in India since Independence.* Ed. by. T. V. Sathyamurthy. Delhi: Oxford University Press, 1998.

Bandyopadhyay, D. "Reflections on Land reforms in India Since Independence". In *Industry and Agricuture in India Since Independence*. Vol. 2. Ed. by. T. V. Sathyamurthy. Delhi: Oxford University Press, 1998.

Behera, Sanjeeb K, ed. *Dalits and Land Reforms in India*. New Delhi: Indian Social Institute, 1999.

Bhaumik, T. K. *The WTO: A Discordant Orchestra.* New Delhi: Sage Pub., 2006.

Brich, Bruce C, et.al, A *Theological Introduction to Old Testament.* Nashville: Abingdon Press, 1999.

Brueggemann, Walter. *The Land.* Philadelphia: Fortress Press, 1977.

Chatterjee, Partha. "Development Planning and the Indian State." In *State and Politics in India.* Ed. by Partha Chatterjee. Delhi: Oxford University Press, 1998.

Chattopadhyay, Manabendu. *Condition of Labour in Indian Agriculture.* Calcutta: K. P. Bagchi & Company, 1985.

Crusemann, Frank. *The Torah: Theology and Social History of Old Testament.* Edinburgh: T & T Clark, 1996.

Dasgupta, Biplab. *Globalization Structural Adjustment Experience.* New Delhi: Sage Pub., 2005.

Datta, Amlan. *An Introduction to India's Economic Development since Nineteenth Century.* Bombay: Popular Prakashan, 1989.

Datta, Bhabatosh. *Indian Planning at the Crossroads.* Delhi: Oxford University Press, 1992.

Dogra, Bharat. *Empty Stomachs and Packed Godowns.* New Delhi: BDPub., 1987.

Desai. A. R. *India's Path of Development: A Marxist Approach.* Bombay: Popular Prakashan, 1984.

Dommen, Edward. *How Just is the Market Economy.* Geneva: WCC Pub., 2003.

Duchrow, Ulrich. *Property for People not for Profit.* London: Zed Books, 1988.

Dyke, Fred Van, et.al, *Redeeming Creation: The Biblical Basis of Environmental Stewardship.* Illinois: Intervarsity Press, 1996.

Ellwood, Wayne. *The Non-nonsense Guide to Globalization.* Cornwall: TJ International, 2005.

____________. *India's Green Revolution: Economic Gains and Political Costs.* New Jersey: Princeton University Press, 1971.

Frankel, Francine R. *India's Political Economy, 1947-2004.* New Delhi: Allied Publishers Ltd., 1978.

Ganguli, B. N. *Indian Economic Thought.* New Delhi: Tata-McCraw Hill Pub., 1977.

George, Susan. *Food for Beginners.* London: Writers and Readers Pub., 1982.

Gurusamy, M. P. "Land Ceiling Acts and Absentee Landlordism." In *Land Reforms in India: Tamil Nadu: An Unfinished Task.* Vol. 9. Ed. by M. Thangaraj. New Delhi: Sage Pub., 2003.

Gandhi, Mahatma. *The collected Work of Mahatma Gandhi* 27th Jan., 1940. New Delhi: Govt. of India, 1958-1984.

Hariss, John. *Capitalism and Peasant Farming.* Delhi: Oxford University Press, 1982.

Jackson, Ben. *Poverty and the Planet: A Question of Survival.* New York: Penguin Books, 1990.

Joshi, P. C. *Institutional Aspects of Agricultural Development.* New Delhi: Allied Pub., 1987.

Joshi, P. C. *Land Reforms in India: Trends and Perspectives.* New Delhi: Allied Pub., 1975.

Joshi, Sharad. *Bharat Speaks Out.* Bombay: Build Documentation Centre, n. d.

Judge, Paramjit S. *Social Change through Land Reforms.* New Delhi: Rawat Pub.,1999.

Kannan, K. P. *Of Rural Proletarian Struggles,* Delhi: Oxford University Press, 1988.

Koch, Klaus. *From Amos to Jesus: Biblical Eschatology and Its Social and Political Implications* . Delhi: ISPCK, 1999.

Komarov, Erik. *Nehru's Views on History as Society and Politics, Jawaharlal Nehru and Reminiscences and Studies.* New Delhi: Streting Pub., 1989.

Kurian, C. T. *Our five Year Plans.* Bangalore: CISRS, 1966.

____________. *Poverty and Development.* Madras: CLS, 1974.

____________. *Poverty Planning and Social Transformation.* Bombay: Allied Pub., 1978.

____________. *The Economy Interpretative Introduction.* Madras: Sage Pub., 1992.

____________. *Global Capitalism and Indian Economy.* Delhi: Orient Longman, 1994.

Lawrence, J. *An Ethical Critical of Land Reform: With Special Reference to the Kerala Land Reform (Amendment) Act, 1969.* New Delhi: ISPCK, 1998.

Leon-Dufour, Xavier. "Introduction: Biblical Theology". In *Dictionary of Biblical Theology.* 2nd Edition. Translated by P. Joseph Cahill. London: Geoffrey Chapman, 1973.

Loren, Wilkinson. *Earth Keeping in the 90's: Stewardship of Creation.* Michigan: William B Eerdamans Publishing Company, 1980.

Mies, Maria. "Capitalist Development and Subsistence Production: Rural woman in India". In *Women: The Last Colony.* Ed. by Maria Mies. New Delhi: Kali for Women, 1988.

Mooij, Jos. *The Politics of Economic Reforms in India.* New Delhi: Sage Pub., 2005.

Namboodiripad, E. M. S. *Economic and Politics of Indian Socialist Pattern.* New Delhi: People's Publishing House, 1966.

Nalunnakkal, Mathew George. *Green Liberation: Towards an Integral Eco-Theology.* New Delhi: ISPCK, 1999.

Nanekar, K. R. *Bhoodan and the Landless.* Bombay: Poular Prakashan, 1973.

Nayar, Baldev Raj. *India's Mixed Economy.* Bombay: Popular Prakashan, 1982.

Noth, Martin. *Leviticus.* London: SCM Press, 1965.

Omvedt, Gail. *Dalits and Democratic Revolution.* New Delhi: Sage Pub., 1994.

____________. *Ambedkar: Towards an Enlightened India.* New Delhi: Penguin Books, 2004.

Rao, VKRV. *Values and Economic Development.* Delhi: Vikas Publications, 1971.

Razu, John Mohan Indukuri. *Global Capitalism as Hydra: A New Look at Market, Money and MNC's.* New Delhi: ISPCK, 2006.

Richardson, Alan. "Biblical Theology". In *A Dictionary of Christian Theology*. Ed. by Alan Richardson. Norwich: SCM Press, 1974.

Rod, G. Von. *Old Testament Theology*. Vol.1. London: Olive Boyd, 1962.

Rudolph, Lloyd I. and Susanne Hoeber Rudolph. *In Pursuit of Lakshmi: The Political Economy of The Indian State.* Bombay: Orient Longman Ltd., 1987.

Seeks, M. Douglas. *God The Economist: The Doctrine of God and Political Economy*. Minneapolis: Fortress Press, 1989.

Sen, Sunil. *Peasant Movements in India.* New Delhi: K. P. Bagchi & Company, 1982.

Sharma, T. C. and O. Coutinhao. *Green Revolution Gaps: A Geographical Analysis*. Jaipur: Rawat Pub., 1989.

Shiva, Vandana. *Staying Alive: Women, Ecology and Survival in India.* New Delhi: Kali for Women, 1988.

____________. *Stolen Harvest: The Hijacking of the Global Food Supply.* London: Zed Book, 2000.

Singha Roy, Debal K. *Peasant Movements in Post-colonial India: Dynamics of Mobilization and Identity.* New Delhi: Sage Pub., 2004.

Smith, Ralph L. "Micah-Malachi". *Word Biblical Commentary*. Texas: Word Book Publishers, 1984.

Turabian, Kate L. *A Manual for Writers of Term Papers, Theses and Dissertations*, 6th ed., Revised by John Grossman and Alice Bennet. Chicago: The University of Chicago Press, 1996.

Van, Drimmelen. Rob *Faith in Global Economy: A Primer for Christians.* Geneva: WCC Publications, 1998.

Vashum, Yahgkahao. "Theology of Land: A Naga Perspective". *The Tribal Worldview and Ecology*. Ed. by A Wati Longcher and Yahgkahao Vashum. Jorhat: The Tribal Study Centre, 1998.

Westermann, C. *Genesis 1-11*. London: SPCK, 1984.

Wilenga, Bastian. *Biblical Perspective on Labour.* TTS: Madurai, 1982.

__________. *It's a Long Road to Freedom-Perspectives of Biblical Theology*. Madurai: TTS, 1986

Wilkinson, Loren. *Earth Keeping: Christian Stewardship of Natural Resources*. Michigan: William B Eerdamans Publishing Company, 1989.

Wolff, H. W. *Anthropology of the Old Testament*. London: SCM, 1974.

Zimmerli, Walter. *Old Testament Theology in Outline*. Edinburgh: T & T. Clark Ltd., 1978.

Articles and Periodicals

Abrece, Savio. "The Struggle Against SEZs in Goa." *Social Action* 58/3 (July-September, 2008): 291-302.

All India Independent Fact Finding Team. "Nandigram Violence, preliminary Report." *Janata*. 62/9 (March 25, 2007): 8-9.

Baru, Sanjay. "Development Alternative." *Religion and Society* 43/ 1 & 2 (March & June, 1996): 70-82.

Bhattacharjya, Satarupa. "Red Terror." *India Today* 33/6 (February 5-11, 2008): 33-36.

Brueggemann, Walter. "The Earth is Lord's-A Theology of Earth and Land." *Sojourner* (October, 1986): 28- 32.

Bunsha, Dionne."Rural Resistance: Gearing up for the Battle." *Frontline* 23/20 (October 7-20, 2006): 9-10.

Chandan, Amarjit. "Victims of Green Revolution." *Economic and Political Weekly* 14/25 (June 23, 1979): 1035.

Collision, J. G. F. "Biblical Perspectives on Stewardship of Earth's Resources." *Bangalore Theological Forum* 18/4 (October-December, 1986): 153-160.

Dalvi, Surekha. "Women Farmers Lead Indefinite Fast Against Reliance Mahamumbai SEZ." *Janata* 62/27 (July 29, 2007): 6.

Das, Prafulla. "Rural Resistance: Tribal Ire." *Frontline* 23/20 (October 20, 2006): 10-12.

Datt, Ruddat. "Special Economic Zones." *Mainstream* 44/47 (November 10-16, 2006):15-19.

Devi, Mahasweta, et. al., "The Public Hearing and Further Investigation on the Struggle by the People of Singur." *Janata* 61/46 (December 24, 2006): 8-16.

Dhawale, Ashoka. "Massive Peasant Rallies Attack Government Policies Leading To Peasant Suicide and SEZs." *Peoples Democracy* 1/28 (October 09-15, 2006): 8-9.

Dutt, Ruddar ."Second Green Revolution." *Janata* 61/ 23 (July 16, 2006): 4-5.

"Factfile, SEZs: Frequently Asked Questions." *Seminar* Vol. 582 (February, 2008): 15-19.

Gopalakrishnan, Shankar. "Negative Aspects of Special Economic Zones in China." *Economic and Political Weekly* 42/17 (April 28, 2007): 1492-1494.

Gopalakrishnan, Shankar. "Signs of an Impending Disaster. "*Seminar* 582 (February, 2008): 25-31.

H. Stek, John. "Salvation, Justice, and Liberation in the Old Testament." *Calvin Theological Journal* 13/2 (November, 1978): 133-165.

Hildyard, Nicholas. "Too Many for What?." *The Ecologist Asia* 5/3 (May/June, 1997): 24-25.

Kabra, Kamal Nayan. "Special Economic Zones." *Mainstream* 44/44 (October 20-26, 2006): 7-13.

Kale, Sampat. "Defeat SEZ Policy." *Janata* 61/36 (October 15, 2006): 8-9.

Kumar, Arun. "SEZ: One more Anti-Bharat Act by India." *The Rally* (May, 2007): 16-19.

Kushal, Debnath. "SEZ Act and CPI (M)." *Janata* 62/16 (May, 2007): 12-15.

M, Soma Sunder. "SEZ and Turmoil in Rural India." *New Age* 56/35 (August 31-September 6, 2008): 5, 12.

Menzes, Ruide. "The Pentateuchal Theology of Land." *Bible Bhashyam (*March, 1986): 4-12.

Mulgi, Sangita. "Special Economic Zone." *Lawyers Collective* (Oct., 2006): 8-15.

Mumtaz, Rifat and Madumanti Sardar."How the SEZ Battle was Won?." *Frontier* 40/36 (March 23- 29, 2008): 7-10.

"No to Forcible Acquisition of Agriculture Land, No to the Land Acquisition (Amendment Bill) Bill." Peoples Voice 30/19 (February 1-15, 2008): 11-12.

"Not Wasted." *Down To Earth* (November 15, 2006): 25-26.

Pachim Banga Khet Majoor Samiti. "Singur: Facts and Untruths." *Frontier* 39/25 (January 7-13, 2007): 7-9.

Party to Launch mass Against SEZs." *Peoples Democracy* 1/28 (October 09-15, 2006): 5-6.

Patkar, Medha and Amit Bhaduri. "Industrialisation." *The Movement of India* 2/2 (March-April, 2007): 6-8.

Patker, Medha, et. al., "UPA's Betrayal." *Janata* 62/12 (April 15, 2007): 15-16.

"Peasant Struggle against Forcible Land Acquisition." *People's Voice* 30/19 (October 1-15, 2008): 8-9.

Piyush. "Contract Farming in India: Death Knell for Farmers." *Lok Samvad* (Sept., 2003): 16-17.

Radakrishna, R. "Agriculture Growth, employment and Poverty: A Policy Perspective." *Economic and Political Weekly* 37/3 (January 19-25, 2002): 243-250.

Rajalaksmi, T. K. "Brave New World of Tax exemptions." *Frontline* 23/13 (July 1-14, 2006): 32-35.

Ramakrishnan, Venkitesh. "Conflict Zones." *Frontline* 23/20 (October 20, 2006): 4-8.

Rao, V. M. "Land Reform Experiences: Perspectives for Strategy and Programmes." *Economic and Political Weekly* 27/26 (June 27, 1992): A 50-62.

Roy, Ashim, et. al., "Smart City, Kerala". *Janata* 62/12 (April 15, 2007): 7.

Sangvai, Sanjay. "This Time Land-Grab by Rich." *The Movement of India* 1/2 (July-August, 2006): 4-9.

Sen, Sunanda."From Import Substitution to Export Promotion: Policy Planning in India's Foreign Trade Sector." *Economic and Political Weekly* 17/14-16 (November 1982): 629-640.

"SEZ Rules Violate Constitution: CITU Petitions Committee On Subordinate Legislation." *Peoples Democracy* 1/28 (October 09-15, 2006): 7-9.

Sharma, Devender. "Displacing Farmers." *The Movement of India* 2/2 (March-April, 2007): 12-13.

Shiva, Vandana. "From Seed to Retail: Globalization Creates Monopolies in Agriculture." *Janata* 61/15 (May 21, 2006): 6-8.

____________.. "New Zamindari and Undermining of food Security in India." *Third World Resurgence* 53/54 (January-February, 1995): 7-10.

____________. Vandana. "South Safeguards Farmers Rights: On Agricultural Biodiversity." *The Ecologist Asia* 5/3 (May/June, 1997): 6-7.

Sidhu, R. S. and Sukhpal Singh."Agricultural Wages and Employment." *Economic and Political Weekly* 39/37 (September 2004): 4132-4135.

Singh, Simpreet. "Sangarsh 2007." *Janata* 62/12 (April 15, 2007): 16.

"Special Economic Zone." *The Rally* (May, 2007): 3.

Srivastava, Muktar. "Foxes have been Let Loose in the Hen House." *The Movement of India* 1/4 (July-August, 2006): 8-15.

Statement made by West Bengal chief Minister, "Buddhadeb Bhattachajee in the state assembly on March 15, 2007." *Janata* 62/9 (March 25, 2007): 10-11.

Suchitra, M. "Prospects for Labour." *Seminar* 582 (February 2008): 36-38.

Surana, Pannala. "Agriculture land Not to Used for N. A Purposes." *Janata* 61/6 (March 19, 2006): 6-7.

Viswanathan, S. and Venkitesh Ramakrishanan." At a Crossroads." *Frontline* 23/24 (December 2-15, 2006): 4-8.

Unpublished Article

Mehta, Jaya. Changing Agrarian Structure in Indian Economy. *Unpublished Article.* 1-17.

Government Document

The Gazette of India (extraordinary Part-II-Section I). *Special Economic Zones* (Ministry of Law and Justice). 2005.

Interviews

Ahamd, Bilal. Market-oriented Farmer. Interview, 10 May 2008.

Ahmad, Aneez. Kondari Village Chief. Interview, 7 May 2008.

Bhatnagar, Anurag. Kunderki Block Officer. Interview, 15th May 2008.

Kannan. Agriculture Labourer. Interview. 16 Sept. 2008.

Pandey, Alok. Assistant Development Commissioner of SEZ Moradabad. Interview, 5 May 2008.

Pandiayan, Market-oriented Farmer. Interview, 14 September 2008.

Rajendran, P. Organizer of Madurai District Agriculture Workers Union Interview, 25 February 2009.

Regina Bai, Adlin. Madurai Pennourmai Iyakkam Office Bearer. Interview, 2 November 2008.

Shanti, M. Madurai Construction Workers union General Secretary. Interview, 4 November 2008.

Singh, Mor. Agriculture Labourer. Interview, 7 May 2008.

Tewar, Ramalingam. Subsistence farmer. Interview, 9 September 2008.

News Papers

The New Indian Express (Madurai), 20 January 2007

The Hindu (Bhuvaneswar), 28 May, 2007.

The Hindu (Banglore), 6 July 2007.

The Indian Express (Chennai), 30 July 2007.

The Hindu (Madurai), 4 January, 2008.

The Hindu, (Bangalore), 7 March 2008.

The Hindu (Madurai), 12 March, 2008.

The Hindu (Madurai), 17 March 2008.

The Hindu (Madurai), 18 March, 2008.

The Hindu (Madurai), 18 June, 2008.

The Hindu (Madurai), 14 October, 2008.

Webliography

"A Congress of Great Resolve for a Big Push Forward." –Featured Paper. http//:WWW.cpiml.org /liberation /year 2008/january/8thparty congress.html. (January, 2009).

"Agitating farmers from Kanjhawala demands denotification of their lands."-- Featured Paper. http://mail.sify.com/readmail. php3? sessid=sicea3ac.(14 October, 2008).

"BJP is likely to support SEZ policy". *Times News Network (26 January, 2007).* Http//: www.times ofindia.indiatimes. com / article show/402189.cms - 65k (5 November, 2008).

"Congress party favours compensating SEZ promoters in Goa". *Economic Times* (19 July 2008). http://www. Economictimes. indiatimes.com/News/PoliticsNation/ Congress_party_ favours_ compensating_ SEZ...in_Goa /.../3252937.cms (5 November, 2008).

"SEZs will affect sovereignty of nation". *Deccan Herald* (26 July, 2007). www.deccanherald.com /CONTENT/Jul262007/district 2007072515174 .asp - 68k (5 November, 2008).

"Uncompromisingly oppose the anti-social SEZ Act! Rights of workers and peasants are inviolable!." *People's Voice* (English Fortnightly) (1-15 February 2007). http//www.cgpi.org (5 November, 2008).

Bidwai, Praful. "India: Special Economic Zones on the Backburner". *IPS* (12February, 2007). 1 of 3, http://ipsnews.net/ news.asp? idnews =36523 (5 November, 2008).

Dutta, Madhumita. "Will Cheyyar be TN's Nandigram?"(6 October, 2008). circular letter to csatts@sify.com (6 October, 2008).

Goswami , Bhaskar. "Special Economic Zones: Lessons from China." –Featured Paper. URL: htt p://en.wikipedia.org /wiki/Special_ Economic_Zones_ of_the_People's_Republic_of_China as retrieved on 18 Jun 2008 03:18:03 GMT. (5 August, 2008).

Interview with Yaswanth sinha by Shantanu Guha Ray. Cited in "Take Jobs to People Don't Take Their Jobs And Force Migration". Bharath Versus India --Featured Paper. www.tehelka.com/story main31.asp? filename=Bu160607 Punditspeak_(16 June, 2008).

Srivastava, Mukta. "Statement on Singur" (3 October, 2008). Circular letter to scats@sify.com (3 October, 2008).

Glossary

Benami Patta	:	registration in unknown name
Benami	:	unknown name
Bhoodhan	:	giving land as gift
Bhoomi Thayi Raitara Samiit	:	The Farmer's Association of Mother Earth
Biga	:	one biga is equal to 6 cent land
Dalit Sangharsh Samit	:	Dalits struggle Organization
Kisan	:	Farmer
Kisan Sabha	:	Farmer's Organization
Krishi Bhoomi Samrakshaka Samiti	:	Save Agriculture land organization
Krishi Bhumi Raksha	:	Agriculture Land Protectors
Madurai Mavatta Vyvasaya Thozhilali Sangham	:	Madurai Agriculture Workers Labour Union
Pachim Banga Khet Mazdoor Samiti	:	*West* Bengal Agriculture Labourer Organization
Pennurimai Iyakkam	:	Women's Union
Pradhan	:	Village chief

Ryotwari	:	Property rights directly to cultivator
Sagh Parivar	:	group Family
Swadesh	:	Local
Zamindar	:	Land Owner

Abbreviations

AICC	:	All India Congress Committe
AIDMK	:	All India Dravida Munneta Kazhagam
AIKS	:	All-India Kisan Sabha
AITUC	:	All India Trade Union Congress
BJD	:	Biju Janata Dal
BMS	:	Bharat Masdoor Sangh
cf. (Confer)	:	compare
CII	:	Confederation of Indian Industry
CITU	:	Central India Trade Union Congress
CPC	:	Communist Party of China
CGPI	:	Communist Ghadar Party of India
CPI	:	Communist Party of India
CPI (M)	:	Communist Party of India (Marxist)
CPI (ML)	:	Communist Party of India (Marxist-Leninist)
DMK	:	Dravida Munneta Kazhagam
DPAP	:	Drought-Prone Area Programmes
DPI	:	
ed.	:	editor
EPZ	:	Export Processing Zone
et al. (et alii)	:	and others
ff.	:	and the following pages

FICCI

HYVP	:	High Yielding Varieties Programme
i.e. (id est)	:	that is to say
IADP	:	Intensive Agriculture Development Programme
IMF	:	International Monetary Fund
INTUC	:	Indian National Trade Union Congress
LPG	:	Liberalization, Privatization and Globalization
MUDA	:	Mysore Urban Development Authority
n. d	:	No Year given
n.p.	:	No publisher given
NAPM	:	National Alliance of People's Movements
NSS	:	National Sample Survey
op. cit (opero citato)	:	in the work cited
PMK	:	Pattali Makkal Kazhi
PRC	:	Peoples Republic of China
RJD	:	Rashtriya Janata Dal
RSV	:	Revised Standard Vision
SEZ	:	Special Economic Zone
SFDA	:	Small Farmers Development Agency
TDP	:	Telengu Desham Party
TRIPS	:	Trade Related Intellectual Property Rights
UPSIDC	:	Uttar Pradesh State Industrial Development Corporation

v., vv.	:	Verse, Verses
WB	:	World Bank
WTO	:	World Trade Organization

Biblical References

Gen	:	Genesis
Exod	:	Exodus
Lev	:	Leviticus
Num	:	Numbers
Deut	:	Deuteronomy
Josh	:	Joshua
Ruth	:	Ruth
2 Sam	:	2 Samuel
1 Kgs	:	1 Kings
2 Chr	:	2 Chronicles
Neh	:	Nehemiah
Esth	:	Esther
Ps.	:	Psalms
Isa	:	Isaiah
Ezek	:	Ezekiel
Mic	:	Micah
Acts	:	Acts of Apostles
2 Thess	:	2 Thessalonians

Index